KIDS & KAOS

Restoring
Calm
Through
Behavioral
Change

Fiona Cattermole,
MSW, CPBA

K I D S & K A O S: Restoring Calm through Behavioral Change
by Fiona Cattermole, MSW, CPBA

ISBN 13: 978-0-9817495-0-1

Library of Congress Number: 2008905799

Cover and Book Design: Nick Zelinger, NZ Graphics

Published by
Fiona Cattermole, MSW, CPBA

Visit our web site: www.kidsandkaos.com

Printed in the United States of America
First Edition

To Lily Rose Schneider,
and her parents Kristen and Paul.
This book is for you.
Happy parenting!

ACKNOWLEDGEMENTS

I could not have written a book about parenting without attributing an enormous amount of what I know to my own parents, especially about the power of unconditional love. I know I disappointed and saddened them at times, but I never lost their love. Not once.

Born in England, but raised in Africa and India, my parents saw to it that my childhood was as normal as it could be had I been raised in my home country on familiar turf. Knowing what I know now about being a parent and living in third world countries, I have at least some idea of how difficult that must have been for them. However, they knew how to meet my needs—especially giving me the boundaries within which I could feel secure—and they allowed me to just be a kid. I do not remember being anxious or confused about what was expected of me. Things were predictable, and I knew how far I could push them before I bounced off one of the limits they had set! Their example has allowed me to pass the gift of unconditional love to my children—Alexandra, Kristen and Josephine—who will pass it on to their children. It is truly the gift that keeps on giving.

These aforementioned children all generously contributed to my current literary efforts by giving me plenty of opportunity to try out a variety of disciplinary techniques while they were growing up. As adults, they have also provided helpful input to this book, for which I am indebted. Through it all, my husband, Paul, walked with me on the parenthood path as, together, we figured out how to raise them, and support one another.

Numerous people have helped me throughout the education, career and business endeavors that preceded, contributed to, and culminated in this book. Two significant mentors who helped me launch my first career and acquire the skills to be a psychotherapist are Ron Travaglione, PsyD, and Shelly Isaacs, PsyD. Among other things, they taught me the importance of active listening and of thoroughly evaluating a situation before being able to help any of my clients. To this day, I rely on those two skills in every relationship I have as a therapist, coach, wife, friend and parent. I also want to thank a special few for supporting the growth of my second career: Bernie Michalek and Leigh Steere for their invaluable marketing advice and Lorna Donovan for always being there with her sales training skills when I needed them. Judy Sabah was instrumental in "birthing" my current coaching career. Michelle Stout has become an indispensable associate, keeping me focused on business development as well as providing valuable information about what it is like to be a parent of young children today. And—to finally accomplish this book—great thanks go to editing and design specialists Melanie Mulhall, Margaret Pevec, and Nick Zelinger.

My appreciation also goes to the many psychotherapy, business and coaching clients I have had the pleasure of meeting. My unique encounter with each one has given me a deeper and broader understanding of human determination and possibility.

Last, but not least, thanks go to my brother, Peter—now deceased—who taught me the importance of writing, and that I should never give up on completing a book once started.

CONTENTS

INTRODUCTION

This book is designed to be a behavioral reference guide for parents of young children ages one through eight. On page 14, you will find a Techniques Index that lists all the techniques contained in the book along with the associated page number for each one. However I caution you not to refer to the Index alone in your rush to remedy behavioral problems. As tempting as that might be, you will get the most benefit by reading the book sequentially first, since each chapter has been carefully designed to give you the necessary understanding and preparation to deal with your child's behaviors in a methodical way. As you read, you can use the Index to quickly and easily find any of the referenced techniques—all of which are capitalized for your convenience.

I have included two chapters not usually encountered in parenting books, but both are crucial in preparing you for behavioral change. The first, Chapter 1, is "Looking Inward: Parental Behavior." This chapter guides you through necessary personal scrutiny as you prepare to influence behavioral changes in your child. It will help you take a close look at certain aspects of yourself, and determine how those aspects support or undermine your parenting efforts. Chapter 2, "How to Parent as a Team," includes an assessment process that can clearly identify different parenting styles, and help parents use the natural differences between them to increase their effectiveness, rather than cause the conflict such differences can create. The assessment results provide a pragmatic approach for discussing differences and remove the emotional baggage that sometimes gets in our way. The remainder of the book takes you progressively through the educational and skill-development processes needed to hone your parenting skills.

Chapter 3, "Looking Outward: Childhood Behavior," covers information about children's psychological and emotional development. Chapter 4, "Laying the Groundwork: Setting Limits and Expectations," covers two essential basics you will need in order to deal with just about any typical behavior encountered in the course of parenting. Chapters 5 and 6 cover the types of behaviors you might want to eliminate, reduce, or encourage, and Chapter 7 outlines specific techniques that will help you do this. Chapter 8, "Establishing Healthy Routines," makes use of everything you have learned and experimented with in previous chapters.

The material I present throughout the book is grounded in the deep compassion I feel towards all parents who commit to the care and guidance of their children until—and sometimes after—they have reached adulthood. I hope it prompts in you the same sense of compassion for yourself and your parenting efforts, as well as for your children.

Sometimes, in our zeal to get parenting right, we become overly controlling of our children's behaviors instead of being in control of *our* behaviors (which is by far the best way to influence change in our children's behaviors.) Therefore, my ultimate goal is to put you in control, to return the reins to your hands if they have come a little loose, and to enable you and your children to experience all the benefits that great parenting bestows.

Another goal is to simplify your job as a parent. As you try out the suggested techniques, not only should you find yourself *doing* less, but you should also find yourself *talking* less. Why? Because talking too much is another common mistake we parents make and in doing so we limit the potential for our children to think and act for themselves. Nowhere is the phrase "actions speak louder than words" more appropriate than for parents.

And, before you begin reading the book, this is the best place for me to clarify what I mean by the words punishment, discipline, and consequences, so that there is no confusion. I do not advocate the use of punishment when disciplining children, because they do not need to be punished. They are not being bad, but merely misbehaving, and I consider misbehaving to be as natural to childhood as breathing. Instead, I encourage you to use an approach to discipline that relies on compassion, leadership and the power of consequences. Punishment implies harsh and negative treatment and does not provide the leadership children need. Consequences occur as a natural result of action taken, are judgment-free, and can be experienced as either negative or positive. Leadership and consequences are much better agents of change than punishment when it comes to children's behaviors.

Throughout the book, I switch between the use of male and female pronouns when referring to your child, and refer to him in the singular for the most part, even though you may have more than one. I have also chosen to refer to parents as partners to accommodate the reality of today's variety of family structures. Partner can refer to anyone who shares parenting responsibilities with you, which could be a spouse, former spouse or former partner as well as a step-parent.

Your behavior will determine whether or not chaos reigns in the home—and also when chaos ends and calm begins. Would you like to end the chaos and enter the calm? If so, read on.

TECHNIQUES INDEX

CHAPTER 1

LOOKING INWARD: PARENTAL BEHAVIOR

There are twelve questions at the beginning of this chapter. Put aside some time to seriously consider how you would answer them. Write down as many answers as you can think of for each question then prioritize your answers. Select the ones that best describe you and your parenting style. Spend some time reflecting on the answers you selected as this enables you to develop a clear picture about how you have influenced your child's behaviors up until now, and how you can influence them differently going forward.

While going through the self-reflection process, you may encounter a few hurdles. For example, you may unearth negative messages from your own childhood, or more recent messages you have received from the media, other parents, family and friends about what a parent should be and do. Consider them all, but only hold on to those messages that are change-promoting, and let go of those that hinder change.

Everyone seems to have a different idea or conflicting advice which adds to the pressure you can feel when examining your own parenting style, habits, successes and failures. Do any of the messages you hear from other sources fit who *you* think you are? If not, ignore them. You know yourself better than anyone else. Listening to conflicting information will only confuse you. One minute you feel like a great parent, the next moment something happens or someone gives you a piece of advice and you feel unsure again. Here are the questions:

1. What kind of parent are you?
2. What kind of parent would you like to be?
3. Do you compare yourself unfavorably to what you hear parents are or should be?
4. Do you consider your parenting style to be strict, lenient, inconsistent, or just right?
5. Do you second-guess, judge or criticize yourself for your parenting style?
6. Do you cast a critical eye on your partner, or other parents?
7. Do you feel pressure to be the perfect parent or have the perfect child?
8. What kind of parents did you have?
9. Do you want to be like them or 180 degrees different?
10. Do you expect your child to obey you happily, put up a fight, or do his own thing?
11. Do your see your child's behaviors as a reflection of how good or bad a parent you are?
12. Do you have a life planned out for your child or are you worried that you do not?

Share your thoughts, questions, concerns and "aha" moments with your partner. It is easy to assume you both have the same expectations about how to parent, but you may actually have some different, and complementary, ideas. You will be better prepared to parent as a team (covered in Chapter 2), once you have gone through this examination process together.

While you take time to reflect on and examine your parenting role and behaviors, do not forget to consider where you got your parenting training. If you are anything like me, and most parents, you did not get any at all. You took on the job of parenting without any training or experience, but with every intention to do it well. What other job carries such responsibility and challenge but requires no training or experience? Despite the lack of training—or perhaps because of it—most parents do an amazing job through sheer effort and commitment to the task.

While you might not have received any official training, you surely received some that was unofficial. No matter how your parents behaved, you will have learned from your experience of them. You may have suffered harsh treatment or severe neglect and have sworn never to treat your child the same way but know of no other way to parent. Or you may remember a childhood that was positive and nurturing and intend to raise your child in just that way. Regardless of your experience as a child, however, being a good parent comes primarily from learning on the job as well as through whatever formal or informal education you pursue on your own, supplemented by coaching and support from professionals and other parents.

Parental Relationship

Your child has an enormous impact on both you and his other parent, as well as on the relationship between the two of you, whether or not you are living together. In fact, if you are no longer together, you may actually attribute the demise of your relationship to strong disagreement and constant fighting over how to raise your child. Whatever the nature of your relationship before your child was added to the equation, his arrival will definitely have had a noticeable impact.

By the same token, the relationship you have with your partner has a tremendously powerful influence on your child. When he is young, the two of you represent 100% of his world, even when he has siblings. In fact, when there are siblings, he will compete for your attention precisely because you *are* 100% of his world, and that competition shows itself in sibling rivalry. When he starts school, his friends and teachers reduce that percentage, but you, as his parents, remain his most important influencers until he finds a partner and has children of his own. Never underestimate the power your relationship with your partner has on him or, conversely, the impact he has on the relationship between the two of you. *Of all the behavioral techniques in existence, the best is the maintenance of a stable relationship between parents.*

In order for you to fully understand how your relationship with your partner impacts your child, it is important to know how he perceives and interprets his environment. During his formative years—up until he is between seven and ten years old—he has an ego-centric view of his world. That is, he can only perceive and understand his world by placing himself at its center. Somewhere between the age of eight and ten he develops the ability to see things from another's point of view and can consider several views other than his own. His natural ego-centricity can easily be misunderstood as selfishness but is actually related to his still developing brain. As he grows and learns and as his brain develops, he will gain the knowledge and experience needed to progress to the next stage.

Another concept for you to understand about your child's psychological development is known as magical thinking. While believing he is the center of his universe, he also believes he has the power to influence what happens to the people in it. His thinking goes something like this: *If something goes wrong, I, or my behavior, must have somehow caused it. If something good happens, it was due to something good I did or thought.* You might see this as faulty logic, but it is actually an important psychological defense mechanism, and as with all defense mechanisms, this one is designed to promote a sense of psychological security. Although he is actually defenseless, he does not know it—nor should he know it—and such an ignorance–is-bliss state provides him with a necessary sense of safety and permanence. His magical thinking allows him to believe that since he can make something bad happen, he can also make it right: he can fix it. He is the master of his universe, and in control of what happens.

Now place your relationship with your partner within the context of your child's ego-centricity and magical thinking. If your relationship is unstable, hostile, or is otherwise in transition, he will think his bad behaviors have caused your arguments and the other things you do that may alarm or frighten him. As a result, he will fix those problems by fixing what he believes is his badness. He will be compliant and fearful of causing trouble. The good behaviors you see may lead you to believe he is an angelic child when, in fact, he is fearful and insecure.

On the other hand, if your relationship with your partner is relatively stable, your child will think it is because of him and will believe in his "master of the universe" powers. He will feel safe and strong. This reduces the chance that anxieties will develop and allows him to behave in a normal, childish way—which is not always compliant!

I am sure you have heard that it is not good for parents to fight in front of their children. What you have just read about the impact of your relationship on your child may help to explain why. However, realistically, you and your partner will fight or get upset with one another in front of him at times. When you do, use it as an opportunity to model conflict resolution. The message he will learn is that conflict happens and can be resolved. If he sees the two of you fighting and you interrupt the fight to continue and resolve it later out of earshot, he will not witness the resolution—which is the most important part for him to experience. Reassure him that your argument (or whatever else is going on that might be distressing him) is not his fault. Tell him in simple terms why it is happening. Be open and honest with him, but spare him too many details.

Give some thought to how your current relationship with your partner impacts your child. If problems such as those described here exist, take the necessary steps to address them.

Compassion

As you parent, remember to regard your child with compassion. He is just a toddler, youngster, or pre-teen who is dealing with a world that requires him to constantly learn new behaviors and adjust those behaviors as required. It is important to accept that his learning curve is mostly vertical, and he is not behaving to annoy or irritate you; he is just making mistakes on his way to becoming an adult. If you see his misbehaving as a direct result of both his natural, childish ignorance and his efforts to learn, you will have an easier time being calm, rational, loving and helpful as you guide him. Even if you do not know any parenting techniques, your compassion will pave the way for a healthy relationship and that is what you both really need.

Fear

You may find it strange to read about fear in a book designed to improve your parenting skills, but before you can improve those skills you first must take a look at anything that could prevent you from making the desired changes. Some common fears parents have center around the issues of discipline and love. If that applies to you, you may be afraid that:

- Your approach to discipline is not strong enough, or it is too strong.
- You will not love your child enough, or will spoil him through loving him too much.
- You will not be able to give him everything he needs to grow up healthy, to succeed and be happy in an adult world.
- You will damage him through lack of parenting experience and do him irreparable harm.

Stuck in an agony of indecision, it is no wonder you may feel the safe choice is to do nothing or live with a permanent wait-and-see attitude.

However, such fears make it hard to be proactive, and can hold you back or stop you in your tracks if you are not aware of them. As you read the rest of this chapter and book, accept the fact that at times your fears may be holding you back. If you are not moving ahead as you would like to, take a small step towards change. If fear is a factor in holding you back, a small step will allow you to move out of your comfort zone, confront your fear, and gradually replace it with confidence.

The Importance of Discipline and Leadership

I have found that both the word and the concept of discipline carry different meanings for different people, based upon their childhood experience. Was discipline harsh, manipulative, unpredictable and frighteningly meted out in your home? Was discipline absent, leaving you unsure and trying to figure things out for yourself? Was discipline consistent, gentle but firm, and predictable? What does the word discipline mean to you? Whatever it means to you, I use the word to mean the firm, gentle, consistent and predictable variety. The best type of discipline is that which provides healthy leadership and the predictable environment children need.

After all, we humans are pack animals and I like to think of parents as pack leaders or Alpha wolves. We can learn something valuable from how the Alpha wolf provides guidance and safety for the wolf pack. He does not sit around trying to get consensus in order to make important decisions. He does not provide pack members with a range of choices about how to behave. When pack members "misbehave" and threaten the safety of the group, they are dealt with immediately, without any warnings or cautions. The need to survive requires absolute and decisive leadership qualities in the Alpha wolf and complete compliance from pack members.

I am aware that you are not trying to survive in the wild and your child will not be eaten by prey if he lacks strong leadership. However, I am

21

making the important point that he needs your leadership in order to feel safe enough to develop the physical, social, emotional and psychological strength necessary to survive and thrive in an adult world. He does not need to be involved in making important decisions for the good of the family, or given numerous choices about what to do from moment to moment, nor will this benefit him. His behaviors cannot be allowed to threaten the peace or healthy functioning of the family. Once he clearly understands what mis- behavior means, he does not need to be given multiple choices on how to behave, or multiple warnings about what the consequences will be if he does not. It is your firm and consistent guidance and follow through that will give him the clear message about how he is to behave.

Perhaps you—like some parents—are concerned that your child will dislike you if you apply appropriate discipline. You may want to be good friends with him and worry that being the disciplinarian will damage that relationship. There is nothing wrong with being a friendly parent. But being a parent who is a friend implies a level of equality that is not healthy or helpful in a parent-child relationship. True, some children resist being disciplined and may react angrily with words that convey the message, "I don't like you." They are either testing your resolve or being honest about how they feel in the moment. Do you ever remember thanking your parents for disciplining you?

You may be a parent who feels guilty that you must put your child in full time or part time daycare so that you can work and contribute to the family income. Your guilt might make you reluctant to discipline or "be unkind" to your child. It is hard to not give in and overcompensate for your guilt, but your firm and consistent discipline is what he needs. One day he may thank you—but if not, you will be proud that you have a child who is able to make a choice about how he behaves, and choose well.

Your child needs the type of discipline I describe in this book. In a leadership vacuum, he may attempt to fill this role for which he is ill-equipped. As long as you are providing the right kind of discipline, know that his complaints are simply a healthy, human reaction. To a child, discipline is a bit like broccoli: although it is good for him, he does not have to like the taste! Just as the receiving end of discipline is not usually fun, neither is the giving end of it…so be prepared.

Whenever I talk about the subject of discipline, I feel bound to say something about shouting and spanking. I know it is unreasonable to expect you to never raise your voice when you are particularly angry or frustrated with your child, but it should not be your usual way of behaving. When you are angry, take a breath, count to ten, drop the subject, or give yourself a Time Out. Do whatever it takes to calm down, because shouting or spanking indicates a loss of control on your part. When you lose control, it is frightening for your child. Not only might he wonder what will happen to him, but he might be scared that nobody is in charge. Be the adult and take the lead.

There is still some public disagreement about whether or not to spank a child and I want to make my position clear on this subject: I do not condone or encourage spanking for any type of misbehavior. Ever. Some parents tell me that spanking works well for them, that they never lose control, and that their children do not suffer. I suspect their children would disagree if they were able to articulate their experience. I have also never heard an adult say they benefited from being spanked as a child. There may be many arguments in defense of the practice, but none of them have convinced me it is a good method to use in guiding behavior in the long term. Admittedly, your child may do what you tell him as a result of your aggression, but he will also fear you and learn to manage his behaviors by avoiding such harsh punishment. What he will *not* learn is how to manage his behaviors from his own desire to be a contributing member of the family and society.

If you are *not* out of control when disciplining, you can select a non-aggressive and nonviolent technique to reinforce or eliminate certain behaviors. If you *are* out of control and yell at or spank your child, then you are reinforcing aggressive behavior. For example, hitting your child while yelling, "I told you *not* to hit your brother!" sends a confusing message. He will read your behavior rather than believe your words, and probably continue to use aggressive behaviors himself, since that is what you are modeling. If you do not agree with my position, I encourage you to experiment with some of the non-aggressive techniques in this book. You may discover that it helps you feel more in control of yourself *and* helps your child feel better about himself and towards you. What have you go to lose?

The Power of Attitude

Just as how you discipline flows from your childhood experience, so does much of your parenting attitude, which can vary from critical to supportive. Whatever your parents' expressed attitudes were towards you, you will have understood their unexpressed ones loud and clear.

Your attitude towards your child can either serve as a powerful deterrent or a powerful motivator, both in changing his behavior and in influencing your relationship with him. Negative attitudes such as preaching, over-talking, or showing impatience, irritability and anger will shut him down, close his ears to you, raise his defenses, and cause him to feel inferior. Positive attitudes such as openness, patience, acceptance, and curiosity about what interests him or is important to him will boost his confidence and serve as powerful motivators to encourage his cooperation.

Example #1: Your child engages in some new and weird behavior or activity. You start off by preaching about how it shouldn't be done, how he should be doing it differently, or how he should be spending his time doing something more productive. He tunes you out because he has a goal he wants to reach, continues what he is doing, and ignores your criticism. Then he makes a mistake. Off you go again, telling him what is wrong with him. Being the creative and motivated human that he is, he continues to tune you out. You notice he is still not listening, so you continue to preach, but now with considerable irritability; eventually showing your anger. Finally he gives up trying to accomplish whatever it was he set out to do and stomps or slinks away to avoid the negativity. You may even tell your-self that he "has an attitude." If this kind of exchange is habitual, it ends with both of you feeling miserable and your child is left with the impression that he has failed—yet again.

Example #2: You show curiosity at his weird new behavior or activity. You are not sure what he is up to, but you are open and have a patient wait-and-see attitude. He is left to explore on his own, and begins to eagerly ex-periment some more. You accept that he is on his own journey and let him continue. This goes on until he reaches some conclusion known only to him—and he is over the moon with the results. His pride is absolute and boosts his confidence. The positive attitude you have brought to the entire endeavor has made you his ardent supporter and he allows you to share in his glory. Now you are both over the moon. If this kind of exchange is habitual, his self-esteem and confidence grow increasingly healthy and solid.

The Power of Voice

What you say is not nearly as important as how you say it. A powerful parental influencer, and one you may overlook, is the way you use your voice. Even if your child does not understand your words, he will under-stand the tone, volume, inflection, speed at which you speak, the mood and timbre, and the overall message your voice conveys. If you tell him he has done a great job with an irritable edge to your voice, he will not trust your sincerity. If he is frustrated and his yelling makes it impossible for him to hear you, your soothing tone will calm him, conveying that someone is in control even if he is not!

Observe yourself for a few days and notice the way you speak to him. Are you calm and clear? Rushed and frazzled? Curious and questioning? Lighthearted and happy? Irritated and angry? Confident and firm? Dismissive and demeaning? Do you speak differently depending on the circumstances or on how you are feeling? As you continue to observe the way you talk to him, try a simple experiment to see if you can change his responses just by changing how you speak. How many ways can you say the same thing and evoke a different response? The results will be interesting and will affirm that you can influence him just by how you use your voice.

The Power of Active Listening

Children need to be listened to—*really* listened to. I am referring to active listening in contrast to normal listening, which is what we do most of the time. When engaged in normal listening, we hear the speaker's words and understand the overt meaning, but sometimes misunderstand any hidden message. The speaker may know we have heard and understood him, or may suspect that we have not, and may or may not come away feeling satisfied with the exchange. *Active* listening does not always come naturally and must be learned and honed like any other skill. Someone engaged in active listening has heard the words and has understood (or seeks to understand) both the overt and covert messages and feelings behind the words. The listener knows he has been both heard *and* understood. Let me illustrate the different impact that normal listening and active listening have on the speaker by the following scenarios:

Today in school your child's friend Bobby was boasting about beating your child's Little League team yesterday. Your child is upset and a little jealous that he was not on the winning team. You listen until he is finished and then say, "Oh I'm sure your team will win next time as long as you practice enough and give it your best shot. But hurry up; we have to get in the car now to be on time for practice. Are you ready?" You have certainly listened and responded, but your child probably feels dismissed, not quite understood, and perhaps a little disgruntled. How do you think he would feel if your response went something like this: "Well, I'm pleased for Bobby, but I can see you had a tough time hearing all about his team's success. You must have felt he was rubbing your nose in it. What a bummer!" That statement conveys that you understand his discomfort, and that it is okay for him to have his feelings. He will get over it more quickly now that you have helped him understand that losing is a part of life.

Active listening can make a huge impact on the speaker. It can calm him down, open him up, and make him feel valued, respected, and cherished. Because it is fundamental to basic communication with everyone, learning and honing this skill is well worth the time it takes.

The Power of Body Language

If what you may have heard about communication is true—that 90% is non-verbal and 10% verbal—then you can accept that body language reveals what you are truly thinking and feeling in the moment. Others will trust you if your body language and your words are congruent and convey the message that, "what you see is what you get." When people pick up mismatches between your words and body language, they will subconsciously trust the non-verbal rather than the verbal message.

Your child picks up an enormous amount of information from your body language. He has been reading and interpreting that language from infancy, just as you have been reading and interpreting his. He can detect whether you are tense or relaxed; emotionally present, approachable and receptive, or pensive and distant. Whatever words you use will not success-fully overrule your body language. Are what you say and how you behave congruent? If you tell your child you are not angry, yet every fiber of your being screams that you are, what do you think he will believe? He will believe that you are angry. If you are feeling tenderhearted and you tell him you love him, will he feel loved? Yes.

As you observe yourself, noting how you use your voice and listen to your child, also take note of what you are truly feeling and how you portray those feelings non-verbally. In order to be congruent, let the way you are feeling guide what you choose to say.

As you can see from this chapter, assessing the impact of your up-bringing, leadership style, attitude, and communication style on your child takes effort and introspection. Make use of a variety of resources when clarifying such things for yourself. Journal your thoughts and ideas, talk to close and trusted individuals, or engage the services of a coach or therapist. Time and effort on such a project will reap great benefit as you bring the best of yourself to your parenting role.

CHAPTER 2

PARENTING AS A TEAM

The Power of the Team

The first chapter was a warm-up for what you are now going to learn: how to parent as a team and how to use your relationship to support your child's psychological and emotional development. Whether you are together, separated, divorced or living in a blended family—as long as you are a co-parent of a child—this section applies to you. The stability of your relationship, consistency in parenting, and unity in leadership offers her necessary fundamental support for healthy growth.

Your child's keen intuition picks up on the atmosphere you create with your partner and the type and level of energy in your relationship. Her ability to consciously make sense of it or to articulate what she senses may be limited and unsophisticated, but she still "gets it." Whenever your relationship becomes unstable—as it does during a brief fight, a prolonged argument, or some sort of transition—she can become alarmed by the instability of the fluctuating emotions and actions around her. Coolness or distance between you and your partner is just as unsettling as a heated battle. She will sense that all is not well in either case. Instability in your relationship signals instability in the care and attention you give her. Her concern, were she to voice it, would be, "Are they able to take care of me properly? Who's in charge? Am I safe? Will I survive?"

When she feels insecure, you will see signs of it in her behavior. Of course, all insecure behaviors are not caused by instability in your relationship.

Insecurity can be caused by something that happened at school, something she saw on television, heard from a friend, or by any number of other external factors. But take a close look at your relationship if you notice any of the following behaviors:

- Clinging to one parent and not wanting to be with the other. (This does not mean she is "blaming" either of you or fears one of you. It just means she senses a rift and doesn't know how to handle it. One of you becomes a safe harbor.)
- She cries, becomes quiet, or hides when you fight or argue. (She is frightened or waiting to see when the coast is clear so she can feel safe again.)
- She whines more often or behaves badly when you are fighting or not getting on well with your partner. (She may be trying to draw attention to herself so you do not focus negatively on one another.)
- Siblings start to fight more than ever. (Again, they may be trying to interrupt your fight by shifting the focus onto them.)
- Changes in her mood, appetite or sleep habits that continue for more than a couple of weeks. (The mood or tone of your relationship may be stressing her to the point of becoming mildly depressed.)

Sometimes it can be helpful to use her behaviors as a barometer for the relationship with your partner. When she is not herself, ask yourself what might be going on with the two of you?

Make sure that your verbal and non-verbal messages are congruent. Intuitively, she understands you. She senses your mood, she can pick up on minute variations in the nuances of your looks, voice and movements, and she knows what it means. You cannot fool her by pretending to be calm when you are anxious or friendly when you are distant. Her ability to know you is a primal and innate ability, a survival mechanism that keeps her safely bonded to you until she is old enough to care for herself.

As she gets older, this ability diminishes. It happens naturally as other distractions in her environment increase, as her independence develops, and as she moves towards her teenage years, grows up, and disengages from you in an appropriate way. But even when she no longer needs you as she did when she was young, your relationship will always benefit from being congruent—meaning what you say and saying what you mean.

Provide her with consistency by keeping her environment structured and predictable since that helps her to feel physically, emotionally and psychologically safe. I am sure you already know how to provide your child with the physical safety she needs. How well you provide emotional and psychological safety depends on how well you understand what those needs are. One of the best ways you can make her environment predictable is to be consistent in how you behave and routine in what you do. The more predictable her environment, the more likely it is that she will develop a sense of security.

Work with your partner to provide a united front, because if you are not united, she is likely to play one of you against the other. She is not being malicious or manipulative when she does this and is probably not doing it intentionally. She may have learned that if she cannot get what she wants from one parent, she might be able to get it from the other. She needs to know that "no" means "no," or "yes" means "yes," no matter which parent tells her. Confusion and misunderstanding abound when parents are not united, so don't let the habit develop.

Working as a team also means that you support, and strive to avoid inadvertently undermining, one other. Different parenting styles can give rise to misunderstandings that escalate, cause misery, and sometimes even result in separation. I frequently hear the following types of complaints from one parent about the other:

- She doesn't listen when I tell her what works.
- She thinks I don't know much about how to be a dad, so I'm not as involved as I'd like to be.
- He lets the kids do anything they want, and they think I'm the bad guy when I crack the whip.
- He thinks it is okay to scream at the kids and I keep telling him it scares them. Then he gets angry because they won't go to him, and he blames me!

Admittedly, parenting problems are sometimes the result of poor communication or lack of skill, but they can also be compounded by differences in parenting style. I have seen many relationships come unglued due to conflicts caused by stylistic differences, since these can be disruptive to the maintenance of stability, consistency and unity that a child needs for optimal development.

I have also witnessed parents who have learned to put their differences to good use, once they have identified what those differences are, and work together as a team. Not only does that level of teamwork improve their parenting, it also strengthens their relationship. I have even seen parents who have left the relationship permanently, yet have managed to reverse the damage that separation did to the relationships with their children. The goal of understanding differences is not to reunite the two of you if you do not want to be reunited, but rather to make life healthier for both of you and your child.

Different Parenting Styles

You and your partner each have distinct personalities and unique ways of thinking and being in the world. As the saying "opposites attract" makes clear, people are often attracted to others precisely because of their differences. If you have ever met a couple with one shy partner and one outgoing partner; or with one partner who sees the glass as half full while the other sees it as half empty, you know what I am talking about.

There is nothing wrong with being different from your partner. But those differences can naturally cause misunderstandings, which, if not addressed, can develop into serious conflict and unhappiness. Not only are you stylistically different from your partner, but your backgrounds are different. As such, you will also have different expectations about how to be in a relationship, how to raise children, and how to deal with such loaded issues as money and sex. What a recipe for disaster! It's a wonder we get along as well and as often as we do.

The DISC© Assessment as a Parent Teaming Tool

When I suggest you team up with your partner, I am not implying that you should change who you are, or change your style of parenting to be more like your partner's. Far from it! It is important that you keep whatever you want—and what works well—of your behavioral style. The teaming approach I refer to requires only that you understand how the natural differences between you play out when relating to one another and when parenting. Such understanding of your differences allows you to agree on how you parent in a stable, consistent, and unified way, while you continue to rely on your naturally different styles.

The material about natural behavioral styles in the rest of this chapter is based on the DISC© assessment tool developed by Target Training International, Ltd. of Arizona. Each person who completes the DISC© assessment receives a twenty-page report that identifies his predominant behavioral style. The dominant style is determined by measuring each of four behavioral factors as outlined below:

- **Dominance:** measures how you respond to problems and challenges.
- **Influencing:** measures how you influence others to your way of thinking.
- **Steady:** measures how you respond to the pace of the environment.
- **Compliance:** measures how you comply with rules and procedures set by others.

Your assessment results indicate whether you have a high **Dominant, Influencing, Steady,** or **Compliant** factor, or some combination thereof. Figure 1 below provides a grid containing a different behavioral style in each of the four quadrants. Each quadrant lists some of the most noticeable characteristics of that factor's style. However, I want to emphasize that any given individual is far more complex and shows more behavioral breadth and depth than demonstrated by his dominant factor alone.

Figure 1: **Behavioral Styles Grid**

Compliant	Dominant
A person with this as their dominant style tends to be seen as:	A person with this as their dominant style tends to be seen as:
Introvert, careful, cautious, detail-oriented, perfectionistic, dependent, controlling, conservative, analytical, reliable, questioning, skeptical, private, thorough and thoughtful, needful of ample time when considering changes. Values quality and excellence above all, sets high standards for self and others, is sensitive to criticism, and conflict-avoidant.	Extrovert, thrill-seeking, forceful, ambitious, determined, controlling, impatient, independent, energetic, task and results-oriented, fast-paced, outgoing, likes challenge, variety and change, a big picture thinker, sensitive to being taken advantage of, easily brought to anger or irritability. The Dominant person does not avoid conflict.
Steady	**Influencing**
A person with this as their dominant style tends to be seen as:	A person with this as their dominant style tends to be seen as:
Introvert, thorough, reliable, patient, loyal, cooperative and collaborative, problem-solver, process and detail-oriented, good listener, teacher and team-player, values privacy, unexpressive, is sensitive to any threats to personal security, and conflict-avoidant.	Extrovert, gregarious, energetic, talkative, optimistic, sociable, trusting, impulsive, playful, loyal, persuasive, good promoter, likes to be liked and trusted, trusting and likeable towards others (sometimes too much so), sees the glass as half full, is highly sensitive to rejection, and conflict-avoidant.

After reading the descriptions of each style in Figure 1, I am sure you can imagine the types of misunderstandings—as well as the potential combined strengths—that might arise from pairing two parents from different quadrants. In the following sections, I describe the typical challenges that various combinations of pairings can face in general, and in parenting in particular. The descriptions also point out the possible benefits of each pairing. All pairings approach stability, consistency and unity in different ways, with no particular pairing having the advantage other than perhaps like pairings (Dominant/Dominant, Influencing/Influencing, Steady/Steady and

Compliant/Compliant). Problems that typically arise due to like pairings are most often caused by competing strengths and by not providing enough variety or counterbalance for the relationship and for the children.

A few words about the introvert/extrovert dimension of the behavioral styles may be helpful to those who are not familiar with the concept. A high score on either the Steady and Compliant factors indicates that you tend to be introverted. A high score on either the Dominant or Influencing factors indicates that you tend to be extroverted. An introvert is someone who derives energy from being alone while an extrovert is one who derives energy from being with other people. This is a fundamental difference in humans, the understanding of which can reap huge benefits, not only in relationship with your partner, but also with your child.

Since I support the notion that "a picture tells a thousand words," I have provided some simple visuals in Figures 2 through 7 below. Refer to each diagram as you read the text below it. The black and gray circles within each diagram represent the dominant, natural behavioral style of each parent pairing being described in the example. Each diagram provides a clear visual that allows you to see how far apart each pairing is. This makes it easier to imagine how distant from, or opposed to, one another you could become on such an intense issue as parenting. As you look at each Parent Wheel Diagram and read the accompanying description, see if you can identify which diagram best describes you and your partner. If the two of you are interested in completing the DISC© assessment and receiving your report and Parent Wheel Diagram, instructions are provided at the end of this chapter. If you are interested in completing the behavioral assessment, but your partner does not want to do so, you can still receive your report and follow-up coaching session to see what changes you can make without your partner's involvement at this point.

Figure 2: **Dominant and Influencing**

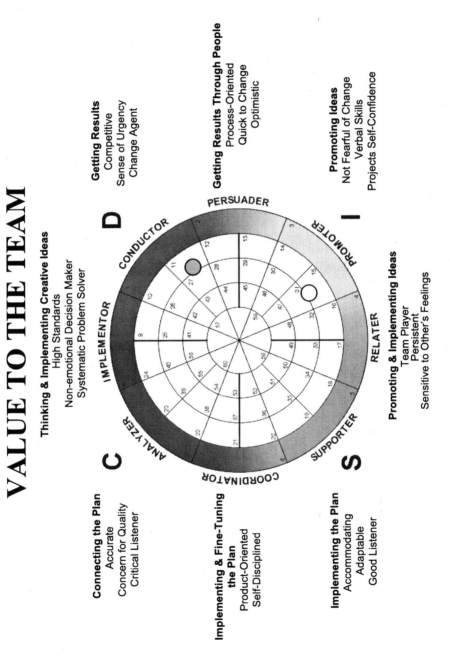

Possible Challenges

When problems occur in the Dominant and Influencing pairing, it is usually because, under stress:

- The Influencing (extrovert) parent can perceive the Dominant parent as pushy, insensitive, a poor listener, controlling, irritable, and/or impatient.
- The Dominant (extrovert) parent can perceive the Influencing parent as too optimistic (a "Pollyanna"), too trusting and open, scattered, overly talkative, conflict-avoidant, and/or clingy.

The Influencing parent might see the Dominant parent as too harsh, irritable or controlling when taking care of the children while the Dominant parent may see the Influencing parent as too soft and unwilling or unable to follow through with discipline.

Parents with this extrovert/extrovert pairing tend to dislike detail work and may fail to follow through or follow up. Both may have trouble meeting deadlines, being on time for appointments, or paying bills. Some level of disorganization reigns in a household run by this pairing which can cause additional friction and stress and make it difficult to establish the kind of solid structure and routine that children need.

Potential Benefits

The Influencing parent can have a wonderfully softening impact on the Dominant parent's tendency to be impatient or insensitive and can help him or her maintain a balanced focus between family, friends and work. The Dominant parent can help the Influencing parent become more focused and pragmatic and less scattered. These two extroverts and their combined characteristics have the potential to invigorate family life with their combined energy, which includes exciting and fun ideas and activities. Their natural ability to see the big picture will make it easy for them to build solid plans for future security, even if they are not always great at following through on the details. Their approach to parenting will be similar in terms of energy and excitement.

Figure 3: **Dominant and Steady**

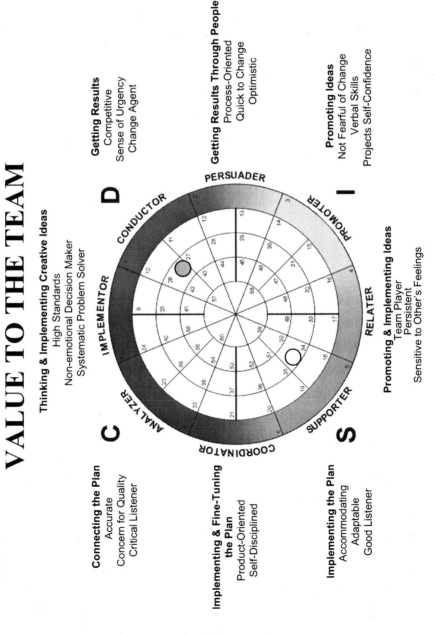

Possible Challenges

When problems occur in the Dominant and Steady pairing, it is usually because, under stress:

- The Dominant (extrovert) parent can perceive the Steady parent as too laid-back and methodical, shy and secretive, not talkative or expressive enough, conflict-avoidant and, at times, stodgy or boring.
- The Steady (introvert) parent can perceive the Dominant parent as pushy, controlling, scattered, impatient, impulsive, and irritable.

This extrovert/introvert pairing approaches parenting, and just about everything else, differently. The Dominant parent wants to raise the children with a good dose of spontaneity, activity and variety, and does not want to spend time on what might be considered boring routine and detail. The Steady parent, who also wants a good life for the children, approaches discipline and activities in a methodical way, attending to all the necessary details before moving on to another topic. The typical conflict in this pairing arises from the differences in their spontaneous versus methodical styles as well as differences in wanting variety and risk versus routine and safety.

Potential Benefits

The pairing of the Dominant and Steady styles has the potential to be especially rich. The Dominant parent can delegate the detail work to the Steady parent, concentrate on keeping the fire of excitement alive in the family, and respect and depend on the reliability that the Steady parent brings to the relationship. The Steady parent can establish calmness, order, routine and structure for the benefit of everyone while indulging, as desired, in the excitement that the Dominant parent brings. However, the successful synergy of these parents' styles depends on their willingness to communicate frequently and openly in order to maintain a solid understanding of their differences and to prevent conflict from entering and damaging the relationship.

Figure 4: **Dominant and Compliant**

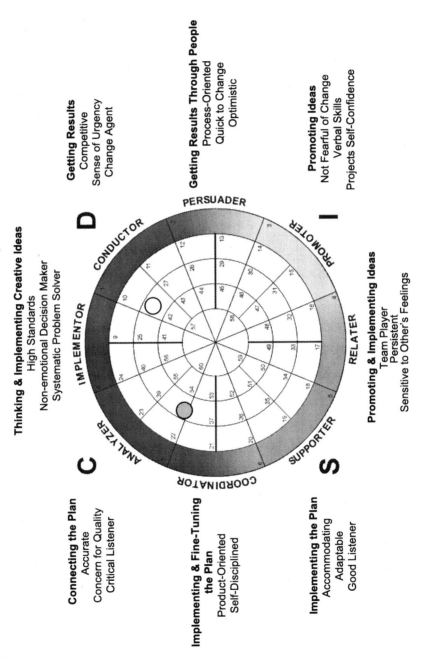

Possible Challenges

When problems occur in the Dominant and Compliant pairing, it is usually because, under stress:

- The Dominant (extrovert) parent can perceive the Compliant parent as picky, asking too many questions and being slow to make decisions or take action, being passively controlling and conflict-avoidant and, in general, not "getting with the program."
- The Compliant (introvert) parent can perceive the Dominant parent as controlling, impatient, irritable, careless, and at times reckless.

These parents constitute another extrovert/introvert pairing whose approach to parenting, and just about everything else, is different. The Dominant parent in this pairing will want to raise the children with a good dose of spontaneity, activity and variety, and will not want to spend time on boring routine and detail. The Compliant parent is determined to establish and maintain neat and tidy order, and wants to teach the children the value of excellence. The Compliant parent is not patient with impulsiveness or carelessness in either the children or the other parent and might feel threatened by the Dominant parent's spontaneity. Unfortunately, this pairing is tough for both parents because the relationship and the children can suffer from inflexibility as each parent clings defiantly to their own behavioral style and tries to control the other. Good communication skills are a must.

Potential Benefits

This pairing can make a dynamite team if they learn to communicate clearly and often. Each must exercise great patience with the other's strengths and decide, together, who gets to control what aspects of the relationship and family life. If the Dominant parent can be patient, the children will benefit greatly from the Compliant parent's ability to instill a sense of value and excellence in them. At the same time, if the Compliant parent can relax and let the Dominant parent indulge the children in energetic and exciting activities, everyone benefits.

Figure 5: **Influencing and Steady**

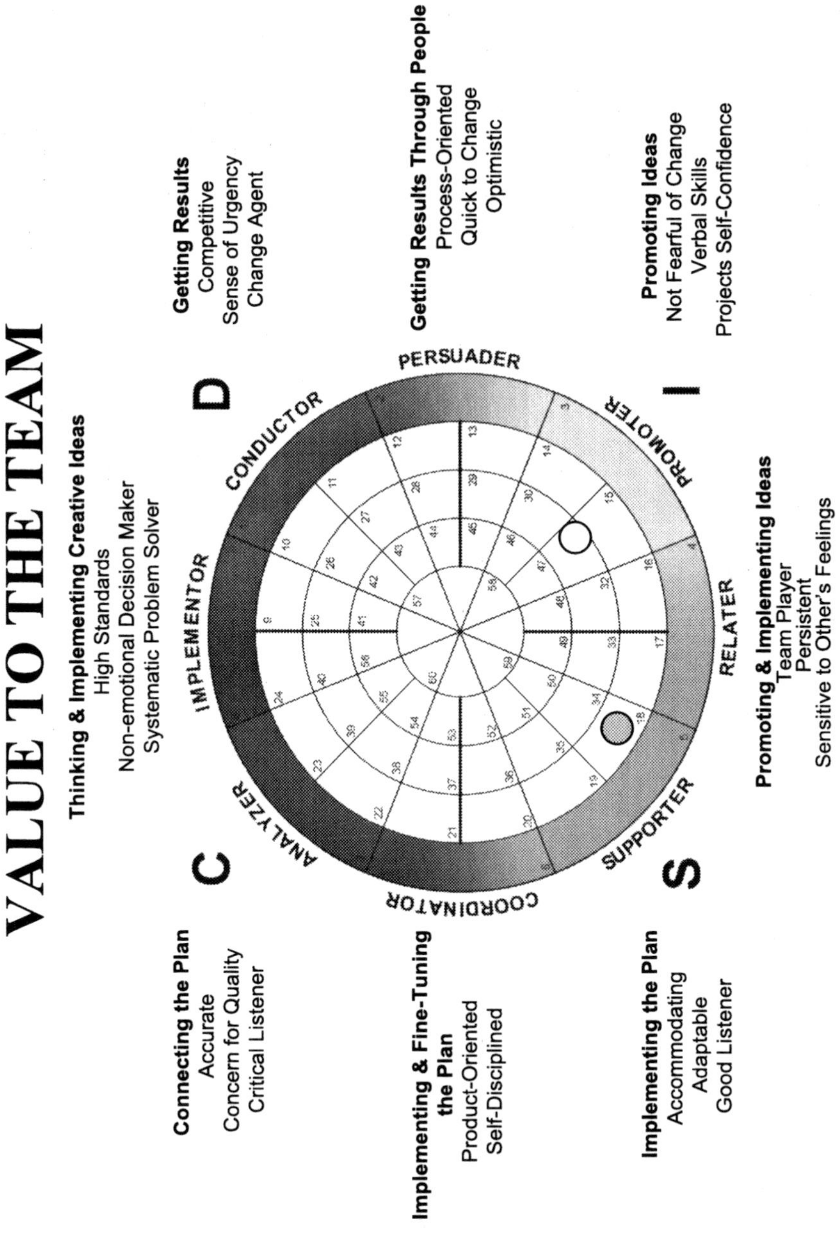

VALUE TO THE TEAM

Getting Results
Competitive
Sense of Urgency
Change Agent

Getting Results Through People
Process-Oriented
Quick to Change
Optimistic

Promoting Ideas
Not Fearful of Change
Verbal Skills
Projects Self-Confidence

Thinking & Implementing Creative Ideas
High Standards
Non-emotional Decision Maker
Systematic Problem Solver

Promoting & Implementing Ideas
Team Player
Persistent
Sensitive to Other's Feelings

Connecting the Plan
Accurate
Concern for Quality
Critical Listener

Implementing & Fine-Tuning the Plan
Product-Oriented
Self-Disciplined

Implementing the Plan
Accommodating
Adaptable
Good Listener

D I C S

PERSUADER CONDUCTOR PROMOTER IMPLEMENTOR RELATER ANALYZER SUPPORTER COORDINATOR

43

Possible Challenges

When problems occur in the Influencing and Steady pairing, it is usually because, under stress:

- The Influencing (extrovert) parent can perceive the Steady parent as too methodical, plodding, unexpressive, and as someone who does not place enough emphasis on having fun.
- The Steady (introvert) parent can perceive the Influencing parent as unreliable, flighty, careless with detail, and not serious enough.

When it comes to parenting, the Influencing parent wants to involve the children in multiple activities and keep them moving along, enjoying the party of life. The Steady parent wants to involve them in fewer activities and spend time relaxing and hanging out, with enough time to complete everything properly. This is another extrovert/introvert pair and, as such, tends to struggle with the differences presented by such a pairing.

Potential Benefits

The Influencing and Steady pairing should have few inherent problems caused by significant stylistic differences, since each has characteristics attractive and similar to the other. Both parents tend to be gentle and tender with the children. Both styles embody many "soft" characteristics and the parents are not likely to become irritable or controlling, nor will they make their children live up to unrealistically high expectations. Children of such couples experience a teaching approach to nurturing, as well as a lively, varied lifestyle. Parents of this pairing should be able to work well together. They are good at reaching compromises because both want to be liked and avoid conflict.

Figure 6: **Influencing and Compliant**

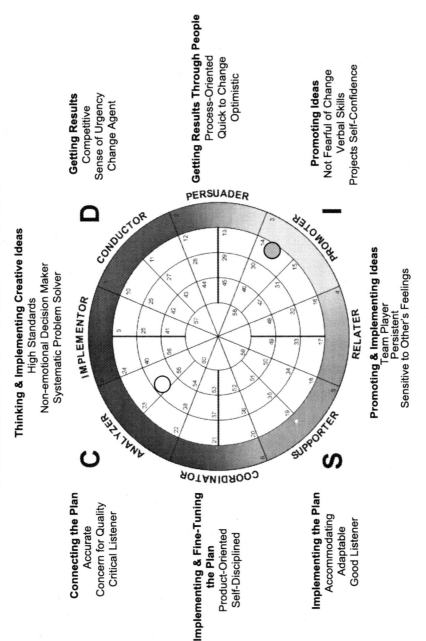

VALUE TO THE TEAM

Thinking & Implementing Creative Ideas
High Standards
Non-emotional Decision Maker
Systematic Problem Solver

Getting Results
Competitive
Sense of Urgency
Change Agent

Getting Results Through People
Process-Oriented
Quick to Change
Optimistic

Promoting Ideas
Not Fearful of Change
Verbal Skills
Projects Self-Confidence

Promoting & Implementing Ideas
Team Player
Persistent
Sensitive to Other's Feelings

Implementing the Plan
Accommodating
Adaptable
Good Listener

Implementing & Fine-Tuning the Plan
Product-Oriented
Self-Disciplined

Connecting the Plan
Accurate
Concern for Quality
Critical Listener

PERSUADER
CONDUCTOR
PROMOTER
IMPLEMENTOR
RELATER
ANALYZER
SUPPORTER
COORDINATOR

D   I   C   S

Possible Challenges

When problems occur in the Influencing and Compliant pairing, it is usually because, under stress:

- The Influencing (extrovert) parent can perceive the Compliant parent as too silent, picky, stodgy; a devil's advocate to all his or her bright ideas and big plans.
- The Compliant (introvert) parent can perceive the Influencing parent as insincere, impulsive, annoyingly bubbly, chatty, and scattered.

This extrovert/introvert pair can easily shut one another out and get into a cold-shoulder rut, since both are conflict-avoidant. The Compliant parent's tendency to be quiet and withdraw from the activity and chattiness of the Influencing parent might make the Influencing parent feel rejected and lonely. That parent will then become even more voluble as he or she attempts to open up the Compliant parent. This pairing can also prove to be a tough one for all concerned. The Compliant parent expects compliance and excellence from the children. The Influencing parent, in contrast, wants them to have a sociable, carefree and active lifestyle.

Potential Benefits

This pairing can also make a dynamite team if they work to hone their communication skills to a fine art, and strive to understand what it is like to be in the other parent's shoes. They also must exercise great patience with the other's strengths. If the Influencing parent can be patient, the children will benefit greatly from the Compliant parent's ability to instill a sense of value and excellence in them. At the same time, if the Compliant parent can relax and let the Influencing parent provide energetic and exciting activities for the children, all will benefit.

Figure 7: **Steady and Compliant**

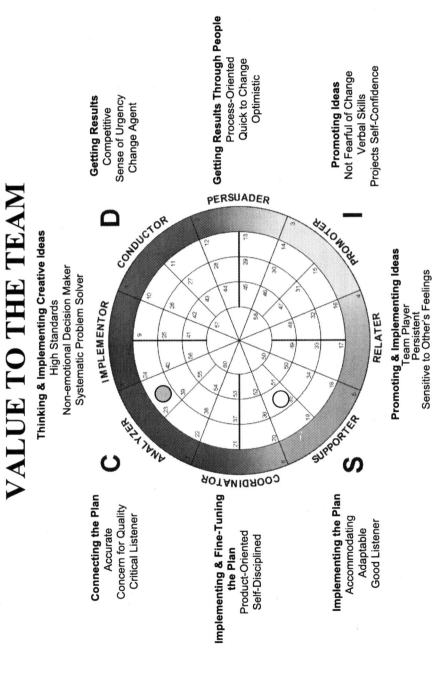

Possible Challenges

When problems occur in the Steady and Compliant pairing, it is usually because, under stress:

- The Steady (introvert) parent can perceive the Compliant parent as too picky, stodgy or critical; sometimes blunt and acerbic.
- The Compliant (introvert) parent can perceive the Steady parent as overly nurturing and may prefer to see more task and results-oriented behavior.

There are usually few relationship problems with this introvert/introvert pairing because the styles similar enough that one can easily understand and identify with the other. However, problems can occur when this pairing parents children who are extroverted and energetic. The children may wear them out easily with their need for excitement and continuous activity.

Potential Benefits

Each parent in this pairing respects the other's desire to be detail-oriented, thorough, calm and peaceful. With either extroverted or introverted children, the Steady and Compliant parents have the natural ability to provide them with great structure and routine, which is always a good thing for their healthy growth.

Communication

The ability to communicate clearly in a relationship between any two people—especially two people who are parents—is vitally important. How you communicate with one another determines the extent to which you both feel understood and valued by the other. Clear and direct communication also increases feelings of trust, rapport and safety between parents and, thus, the children. Good communication can help a relationship almost more than anything else.

Perhaps from reading the previous section, you have identified your style as a parenting pair. If so, you will find the Communications Tips in Figure 8 helpful. If you think you are best described as Compliant, and your partner is best described as Dominant, use the tips from the Dominant section to guide you on how to approach him or her on a current or typical problem, and see if it helps. You may get a lot further in your discussion than you have in the past.

Figure 8: **Communication Tips**

Compliant	Dominant
When communicating with a person who is (Compliant) dependent, neat, conservative, perfectionistic, careful and compliant: • Prepare your case in advance • Stick to business • Be accurate and realistic Factors that will create tension or dissatisfaction: • Being giddy, casual, informal, loud • Pushing too hard or being unrealistic with deadlines • Being disorganized or messy	When communicating with a person who is (Dominant) ambitious, forceful, decisive, strong-willed, independent and goal-oriented: • Be clear, specific, brief and to the point • Stick to business • Be prepared with support material in a well-organized "package" Factors that will create tension or dissatisfaction: • Talking about things that are not relevant to the issue • Leaving loopholes or cloudy issues • Appearing disorganized
Steady	**Influencing**
When communicating with a person who is (Steady) patient, predictable, reliable, steady, relaxed and modest: • Begin with a personal comment – break the ice • Present your case softly, non-threateningly • Ask "how?" questions to draw them out Factors that will create tension or dissatisfaction: • Rushing headlong into business • Being domineering or demanding • Forcing them to respond quickly	When communicating with a person who is (Influencing) magnetic, enthusiastic, friendly, demonstrative and political: • Provide a warm and friendly environment • Don't deal with a lot of details (put them in writing) • Ask "feeling" questions to draw their opinions or comments Factors that will create tension or dissatisfaction: • Being curt, cold or tight-lipped • Controlling the conversation • Driving on facts and figures, alternatives, abstractions

Conflict

Not only will the information contained in the **Behavioral Styles Grid** in Figure 1 and the **Communication Tips** in Figure 8 help you and your partner communicate more clearly, it will also improve your ability to deal with conflict. Unfortunately, many of us prefer to avoid conflict rather than meet it head on, because we have never been trained *how* to deal with it. Even for people who unhesitatingly engage in conflict can become overbearing and aggressive because they often have not learned how to express themselves appropriately. In fact, because the majority of us prefer to avoid it, we are frequently left with few choices for resolving conflict. In the face of open hostility or even strong disagreement, it is tempting to bury things under the rug, which only makes matters worse.

Before trying some of the ideas presented in Figure 8, consider completing the DISC© assessment and generating your own Parent Wheel Diagram. Instructions on how to do this follow. After reviewing your results, take advantage of my complimentary forty-minute telephone coaching session to see how you can use them to improve your relationship and ability to parent as a team.

Although the material in this chapter covers how to parent as a team, there are some situations where this is just not possible, nor at times even appropriate. Perhaps one parent is simply not interested in teaming up, or makes a conscious decision *not* to team up. Both positions should be respected. Nobody should be forced into playing on a team. If your partner is not willing to work with you as a team, all is not lost. One parent can make a significant difference simply by interrupting old patterns of behaving. Changing one part of a system has an impact on all other parts of the system according to Systems Theory. It only takes one parent to make changes. So don't give up.

Assessing Your Partnership & Developing Your Parent Wheel Diagram

1. Send an email to **assessments@kidsandkaos.com**. You do not need to write anything in the body of the email unless you have a question or comment you would like to add.

2. Once your email is received, you will be contacted by return email (if there are no other instructions in the body of the email) to arrange a complimentary, forty-minute debriefing telephone appointment (should you want one) along with instructions on how to prepay the assessment costs.

3. Once the appointment has been scheduled and prepayment received, you will be directed to a website and given a log-in code and instructions on how you and your partner can complete your assessments.

4. Immediately upon completion of your assessments, you will each receive your report and Parent Wheel Diagram.

5. During the telephone appointment, the significance of your differences will be explained to you in your current context, along with any questions you may have about how to make the most of your differences, both in your relationship and as parents.

CHAPTER 3

LOOKING OUTWARD: CHILDHOOD BEHAVIOR

Now that you have spent some time reflecting on the type of parent you are, and would like to be, you are ready to take the next step in effecting behavioral change in your child and deepening your understanding, if necessary, about why he behaves the way he does.

Your child behaves for a reason—and he also *misbehaves* for a reason. The distinction between behaving and misbehaving is totally lost on children until they are old enough to have learned the difference through experience brought about by your guidance.

Your child behaves because he has learned that certain behaviors result in his getting what he needs, likes, or wants and that other behaviors result in his avoiding what he *does not* like or want. What need, want, or like he is trying to satisfy or avoid might not always be readily apparent, but rest assured that he is behaving for a reason, not for *no* reason. I know of no purposeless behavior in a child experiencing normal development. It is up to you, as his parent, to do what it takes to understand his needs—as demonstrated by his behaviors—and respond to them as best you can.

Behavior as Communication

Your child uses behavior to communicate—the younger and more pre-verbal he is, the more he will use behavior to communicate with his world. It makes sense to assume that his behaviors are efforts at communication rather than an indication of his goodness or badness Your task as a parent is to learn his behavioral language as well as you can, and interpret it as accurately as possible. It is sometimes easy to jump to the conclusion that your four-year-old is being rude or fresh when he shouts out "You're mean and I don't like you!" and punish him for his outburst. Perhaps he is angry or upset at something you have asked him to do, but has not yet learned to contain his emotions or use his words to appropriately express himself. You can still let him know, kindly, that you do not want him to talk that way, but you understand he feels angry about something and you will happily help him out if you can. This way you contain him (with your calm, kind voice), and provide a word (angry) that he can use the next time those same feelings arise.

Behavior as Symptomatic

Poor behaviors in your child should also be seen as symptoms; as outward manifestations of possible inner distress. Physical symptoms frequently alert us to our body's internal dysfunction or poor health. We would not become impatient or angry towards a rash that kept breaking out, or a recurring pain. Rather, we would look for and treat the root cause of such symptoms and treat the cause, rather than treating the recurring symptom. Your child's hunger or tiredness can bring on surprisingly poor behavior. If you think either factor may be the cause of his poor behavior, why not prevent the problem by making sure his meals are regular and nutritious, and that he has a regular bedtime that allows him ample time to sleep? If you find that he is behaving differently than normal, and you are unable to find a root cause, consider asking an experienced parent or professional what might be going on and what you can do about it.

This is a good place to mention the behaviors-as-symptoms you may see in a child who feels insecure or fearful as opposed to one who feels safe and secure. When behaving out of fear, a child rarely questions anything, but simply complies, whether he wants to or not. He becomes anxious when he makes a mistake out of ignorance or inexperience, and may try to avoid punishment by lying or being sneaky. He may be quiet and speak only when spoken to or speak only when telling you something he thinks you want to hear. His behaviors appear contained and adult-like, but he may frequently look guilty or ashamed as he senses he has done something that displeases you. He may seem to be the perfect child, but he is a frightened child and needs your understanding.

The child who behaves well from a sense of security exhibits behaviors that are all over the map: from quiet, pensive, curious and predictable, to wild and crazy, loud, boisterous, funny, and goofy. He takes his mistakes in stride, though he may get frustrated. He asks for help when struggling, says what is on his mind whether or not it is popular with the adults around him, and generally acts like a free spirit. That's because he *is* a free spirit. If the secure child lies, cheats, or is sneaky, it is more likely that he is behaving like that to *get* something he badly wants, rather than to *avoid* harsh punishment. He has learned that his punishment (given as positive discipline and leadership) fits the crime and is fair. He may not welcome discipline and may grumble about it, but he is not afraid of it, nor is he afraid of you.

Childhood Needs

Your young child uses behaviors as a way to express his needs. The younger he is, the more his cries and other behaviors, convey them. His cries can communicate a variety of meanings, so from birth, there is a surprising amount of relating going on.

As he gets older, he uses more sophisticated methods, such as increasingly articulate verbal communication, writing, facial expression and body language. Whether young or not so young, he behaves the way he does for one or more of only a few reasons:

- **Safety:** He needs to feel/be physically, emotionally and psychologically safe.
- **Physical needs:** He is hungry, thirsty, hot or cold, or tired; he feels the discomfort of gas or the need to eliminate.
- **Emotional and psychological needs:** He needs affection, recognition, or nurturing; he is frustrated, frightened, angry, or sad, or is overwhelmed by some other emotional stimulus.
- **Cognitive needs:** He is curious, intelligent, and a natural learner and may be over or under-stimulated by his surroundings; he needs direction and guidance.
- **He has parents (!):** His behaviors are shaped by your reactions to his behaviors.

Example: His natural curiosity leads him into trouble, such as climbing onto a table from a chair when he is fifteen months old. You suddenly see him, react with horror, and rush over to take him down. He is alarmed by your body language, facial expression and by whatever choice words and phrases fall from your astonished lips. What is his experience of your reaction? Probably alarm, just like your reaction. Now he has learned that this particular behavior (climbing up on things) gets an alarming reaction from you. That might deter him from doing it again, but if he really wants your attention the next time your focus is elsewhere, guess what he might do? Yes, climb right up on that table again! Little do you realize that you have just taught, and reinforced, that climbing behavior! Parents have a powerful influence—both good and bad—on their child's behaviors.

Parents often unwittingly *cause* undesirable behaviors. In fact, you directly or indirectly influence every behavior your child develops. The good news is that if you can *cause* him to behave in an undesirable way, you can just as easily *cause* him to behave in a desirable way. My point, and one of the main points of this book, is that you have the control to change what you see as undesirable. The reins are in your hands, just where they belong. You are in control.

What I have just said reveals my philosophy about parenting, developed through years of professional practice and personal experience. You have to make changes in the way *you* behave in order to get your child to make changes in the way *he* behaves. Although this may sound like you are being held accountable for his behaviors, it is not entirely the case. Yes, he can—and should—be held accountable for his behaviors once he has learned how to behave, but you are the one who must first teach him *how* to behave. If he is behaving badly, either he has not been taught how to behave well, or he is not receiving the guidance he needs to maintain his good behavior.

Parents who attend my presentations and workshops usually have an "aha" moment when I make the point that they can—and must—be in control. When this happens, they become even more committed to the process of change—*their* attitudinal and behavioral change—for the benefit of their child. Some parents, however, have become so dismayed by their child's behaviors that they have little energy or motivation left to make any changes. They feel unable to commit to the process of change. If you happen to be at this point, take heart and keep reading. The guidance in this book is designed to free up your time and energy and empower you to become an effective parent. It may encourage you to know that there are no behaviors so dismal that you cannot make some positive difference by changing how you respond to them.

As you prepare to make changes, the following section on childhood psychological development may prove helpful when it comes to understanding why your child sometimes behaves poorly. The last part of this chapter includes two critical topics worth addressing when it comes to influencing change in his behavior: time and nutrition. How you manage time and nutrition (both yours and his) will have a direct impact on how he behaves or misbehaves.

Childhood Psychological Development

Parents are generally exposed to more information about what physical changes children go through at given ages than they are about the psychological or emotional changes. This section serves to fill that gap by giving some basic facts concerning children's psychological, emotional, and social development. The stages described are sequential, and ideally, should be completed that way. However, each stage can be completed positively or negatively, either promoting healthy growth or resulting in some developmental deficit.

The likelihood that a child will positively complete each stage depends a great deal upon the type of parenting and nurturing he gets. The material below describing each stage is taken from research developed and published by psychoanalyst, Erik Erikson, in the 1950s. Although Erikson actually detailed eight stages of psychosocial development covering the lifespan, I am only presenting the first four, which cover the childhood years.

Age Birth to Two: Basic Trust versus Basic Mistrust in the Environment

Your child is learning all about his environment from the moment of birth. Whether he can, and how consistently he can, rely on your responsiveness to his needs will inform him how safe or unsafe his environment is. The safer he feels, the more trusting he will be. If he receives inconsistent, inadequate or irritated parental attention, he will likely experience insecurity and develop a sense of mistrust.

I am sure you have heard of children in orphanages and homes who end up looking physically wasted and acting psychologically, emotionally and socially starved due to inadequate attention and care. Such children have learned their environment is unreliably responsive—or essentially non-responsive—to their needs. Sadly, they have given up trying to get attention. They suffer from a deep and pervasive loss of hope that leads to their failure to thrive. If left in a state of neglect like this until they are about five years old, they cannot attach or form a relational bond with another human, even when adopted into a loving and nurturing home. So great is the need in our species for nurture and attention that a lack of it can even cause death.

This extreme is not one you are likely ever to face as a biological or adoptive parent, because, born into society as we know it, your child is probably well cared for and will develop a sense of basic trust in his environment. In fact, parents in most known societies are highly committed to attending to their children's needs and make sure that hunger, thirst, pain and discomfort are quickly alleviated. This kind of nurturing supports the development of a sense of hope and optimism, and the knowledge that he lives in a benign and nurturing environment, one upon which he can depend.

Even if you leave your child to cry himself to sleep—once assured by his doctor that his caloric intake is sufficient to allow longer times between feedings—you will not disrupt his sense of trust if his other needs are consistently met. Sleep training, when appropriately done, causes no harm.

When he is about a year old, he will probably show signs of separation anxiety by protesting at being left in someone else's care. He is not being neglected, and will not suffer from being left with an unfamiliar, responsible adult. Separation anxiety is a normal and necessary part of his development. He is beginning to realize that he is a separate entity, and separation from you can be frightening until he gets used to it. When you must leave him with another caretaker, do not let this transitional behavior concern you. He will be happy to see you when you return.

Soon after experiencing the transition from being completely dependent as an infant to having separation anxiety as a toddler, he develops confidence in being a separate person as he enters the "powerful twos" stage—which can start around eighteen months, or even younger. He learns to flex his independence muscles, and saying "no" makes him feel *so* powerful that he will say it often! What is sometimes seen as outright defiance (and what has contributed to the negative label "terrible twos") is actually just your child practicing his newfound and immature independence. He is far too young to understand the concept of defiance, let alone intentionally behave defiantly. But he can be taught to be defiant in reaction to the way *you* behave, so be careful how you react to his displays of nascent independence.

The best way to handle what appears to be his defiant or oppositional behavior at this naturally curious and explorative stage is to redirect him rather than oppose or sanction him. Instead of telling him not to do things (which can so easily make him resistant), redirect him to things you would rather he do. He will probably transfer his curiosity to something else and be just as happy. If you must tell him not to do something for his safety, keep your voice kind, and tell him why in *simple* terms. The only behaviors you should redirect him from are those that jeopardize his safety or show aggression towards others. (You will find more on toddler aggression in Chapter 5.) He cannot be expected to have any social graces yet—like saying "thank-you," "please," or "sorry"—so do not expect or require those behaviors from him just yet.

Ages 2 to 4: Autonomy versus Shame

Building on the beginnings of the independence he developed in the first of Erikson's four stages of development, your child will need opportunities in the second stage to learn new skills and behaviors that bolster his sense of mastery and accomplishment. Also, as his young identity continues to develop, he begins to use the word "me," since he can sense that now there is a "me" as distinct and separate from a "you."

Support both his growing identity and urgent desire to accomplish new skills by encouraging him to try out a variety of things, even if it does occasionally result in a bump on the head as he learns about his physical abilities and limitations. The more he is allowed to accomplish, the prouder he will feel. If he is frequently told "no," or his attempts at something new are constantly interrupted and thwarted, he may give up trying and become timid and dependent. Rather than developing a sense of pride in his accomplishments, he will develop a sense of shame in his inadequacy and only tentatively try something new if strongly encouraged. A quiet, polite or adult-like child at this stage should be cause for concern, since such characteristics and behaviors are not age appropriate.

Ages 3 to 6: Initiative versus Guilt

Successful achievement of the first two stages will prepare your child well for the third of Erikson's four stages of development, which he enters with a sense of trust in his environment and confidence in his ability to master new things. The third stage requires him to focus on developing his imagination, engage in active play with his peers, cooperate with others, and learn how to lead as well as how to follow. If he takes advantage of the opportunities offered during this stage, he will come through it with the beginnings of the ability to share, play fair and take the initiative on simple issues.

Help him develop the social and emotional skills during this time by making sure he is exposed to children his own age through day care, pre-school, or play dates. Be patient with him as he struggles to let go of his toys while learning to share them. Let him experience taking his place in line and waiting his turn. Expect some mistakes and failures, but continue to guide and encourage him.

Unsuccessful progression through the first two stages means he enters this stage with a deficit. He may feel distrustful of his environment, and his previous lack of success in mastering new things may lead him to feel that he is a failure. These developmental deficits might hinder his ability to enter into and benefit from group play. This in turn deprives him of the plentiful opportunities he needs to develop his imagination, as well as learning to give and take, play fair, negotiate, to play on a team, lead, and follow. He will be comfortable with adults, yet not socially adept with his peers, and as such may feel different from, and be perceived as different by, other children. He may either act aggressively towards his peers or withdraw from groups. The socially undeveloped child should not be confused with a child who is naturally shy, who will, after observing others in the group, eventually join in and engage appropriately with them.

Age 6 to 12: Industry versus Inferiority

Building on the successful completion of the previous three stages, your child is now ready to develop peer relationships and play according to the rules of structured activities. He knows how to team up with others and has developed self-discipline and needs less monitoring. This adds to his sense of autonomy and independence. In addition, he applies his skills to master academic subjects such as social studies, reading, and math. At this time he is introduced to the great societal and academic measure: grades. His natural tendency is to work hard to master the new material and, if adequately taught, can be spectacularly successful. However, he can be made to feel inferior if his grades are poor and he is berated or put down, rather than given help to keep up. Poor grades indicate that he is struggling and not a laggard! He needs help so his efforts can pay off and he can regain his sense of mastery and pride. Ideally, grades, and other measures of success at this age should be given for effort, not results.

Whatever your child's age, one way to get a better understanding of his psychological needs is to imagine what it is to be his age. Imagine how small and insignificant you are at the age of four, for example. Everyone else around you is a giant. Your neck is always craning upwards to communicate with adults and you are constantly being told what to do, how to do it, and what not to do. Does anybody ask for your input? If you make suggestions, do they hear you or respond? You cannot do as much as the adults, like drive a car or even ride a bike. You cannot reach many of the things in your house and are reliant on older people to take care of just about everything. At the same time you are full of energy, drive and enthusiasm and want to try everything that everyone else does. You get frustrated when others hold you back, or when they get impatient with you and do not take time to teach you new things. You do not know as many words as they do, so when you *do* get frustrated, you cannot always make yourself understood. How powerless and helpless this can make you feel.

Imagine being the same four-year-old, yet somebody cares about what you are saying. They ask you to show them what you mean and they show curiosity and delight in it. They encourage your efforts to learn something and they help you, but they do not do it for you. Your accomplishments are totally yours and you know it! Don't you feel powerful? Doesn't it make you want to do more, be more helpful, show everyone what you can do?

Now apply all of that to your child. How can you support the development of a greater sense of accomplishment and pride in him? Whatever his age, take a few moments to put yourself in his shoes. Be him as much as you can be. This will help you understand what he needs, how to guide and help him, how to champion and encourage him, and how to let go and watch him grow.

Making the Most of Time

I could write a book about time and how we use—and misuse—it. And while this book is not about time management, it is important to mention it because time is critically important to parenting and effecting behavioral change. Whenever I give a presentation to a group of parents or conduct parenting classes, the topic of time, and how to fit everything into twenty-four hours a day invariably comes up. Here are some truisms about time management as it applies to parenting:

- There is little point in learning about even the most effective parenting techniques if you do not make time in your life to apply them.
- When you are pressed for time, you are less patient and less able to deal with the many problems that pop up and demand your attention. This only increases the stress as the problems do not go away.
- When you try to fit too many activities into too little time, you accomplish less, adding to your sense of stress.

Your child's behaviors can be directly impacted by how much time he has for sleeping, relaxing, and getting things done—and by the behavior of his time-starved and stressed-out parents! A tired, cranky child (or, for that matter, a tired, cranky parent) can make family life miserable. There is no behavioral technique that will cure your child of his cranky behavior other than sleep, so give him plenty of it and you will keep any crankiness to a minimum.

Although you may desperately want spare time in your day, it may be difficult for you to get it unless you are prepared to make some tough choices. If you are not already good at doing so, say "no" to avoid over-committing yourself to extra work or to school and volunteer activities even though you may feel you are letting people down. You will appreciate the benefits of setting limits to the demands on your time.

What time management ultimately comes down to is setting priorities and improving efficiencies. You and your partner can take advantage of the differences in your parenting styles by drawing on your complementary strengths. As you set priorities, remember that there is always a great deal of social pressure to provide endless activities and opportunities for your child. Those activities, coupled with homework and family time, can become burdensome when you must fit them into the few hours each day that are available. To remedy this, I suggest you schedule white space (unplanned or unscheduled time) on your calendar. However, when you decide to cut something out of the schedule to make room for white space, *what* you cut will likely be unpopular with someone. You must be determined to make the necessary changes or you will cave in. Here are some suggestions that might be helpful as you plan to manage your time and use it more efficiently:

- Let the parent who is better at detail see where he or she can prioritize, organize, and make better use of available time.
- Put plenty of white space on your calendar. It will not remain white space for long. Use it to relax, hang out with your child, do something else you enjoy–or nothing.
- Make an early bedtime for your child a top priority and keep it at the same time every night. Make sure he gets all the sleep he needs. If other plans tend to get in the way and make him late for bed, drop the other plans, even if it is compulsory softball practice. It will be worth it in the long run. Use the time after he is in bed and before you go to bed to do something that relaxes or nurtures you.
- Prioritize getting enough sleep for *you*, too. Not only will you be a better model for your child, but the energy you gain from

being well rested will actually help you make more efficient use of your time.

- If you are involved in multiple after-school activities, drop one after-school activity per child per week.
- Develop better routines at home (Chapter 8 deals with this). Routines not only save a lot of time, they also improve the mood in the home because, once established, they eliminate the need to help, monitor, or nag at every step of the way.
- Expect—and accept—help from all family members. Is one person doing too much and not delegating? Is everyone taking enough responsibility for themselves?

Continue to search for extra time. It will be there if you look for it hard enough, and available if you want it badly enough.

Another important reason to make the best use of your time and not over-commit yourself is that your child needs your undivided attention. As little as ten to fifteen minutes with you each day will probably eliminate many of his annoying behaviors. The time you spend completely focused on him helps build his self-esteem. When faced with making a choice between giving him more of your time, exposing him to another athletic or school-related activity or social event, choose time with you.

Understandably, freeing up time is easier said than done, especially if you and your partner are working full time. Where can you find an extra ten to fifteen minutes? And how can you keep your attention focused when you have a laundry list of to-do items rattling around in your head? Finding the time and staying focused may be hard to do at first, but once you are committed, it will get easier. If you are distracted by your to-do list, make sure you have an activity to focus on with your child, so you can be fully present. Do something he likes, such as reading together, playing a card or board game, or going for a bike ride. Since your brain can only focus on one thing at a time, this will prevent it from wandering to the to-do list. Try it for a week and see what happens.

Nutrition, Sleep and Exercise

In addition to changing the way your family uses its precious time, be sure your child is getting ample quality nutrition, adequate sleep and sufficient physical activity. Admittedly, whether you eat out or at home, food preparation takes time. But grabbing food on the run, dashing through the drive-through on the way to a game and eating in the car, or rushing through hastily prepared meals at home all adds to the family stress. The same hectic schedule that causes us to eat that way is the same culprit that tends to eat into the time we put aside for sleep. As a culture we shortchange ourselves on both sleep and nutrition, giving neither the priority they deserve. There are few cultures that do that. In fact, both food and relaxation are given top priority in many other western—and eastern—cultures.

In recent years, numerous studies have shown that a lack of sleep and poor nutrition are two highly significant contributing factors to the growing problem of obesity and obesity-related conditions and illnesses in our culture. Study results have also long shown a connection between food and its impact on mood and behavior. Chemical additives, sugar and many ingredients found in highly processed foods are known to affect children's behaviors. When it comes to activity, simply encouraging your child to play (riding a bike, playing an active game outside) rather than watch TV or engage in other sedentary pursuits will make a difference to his health. As much as weather and other conditions allow, make outdoor rather than indoor activities a habit.

Through the choices you make, you can have a direct, positive impact on your child's health. When you provide the appropriate nutrition, relaxation, and exercise to meet his growing needs, he will glow with health instead of becoming an obesity-related statistic. If you need to, use some of the time you free up for yourself to become educated about his nutritional needs, as well as his need for sleep and exercise. Many helpful, free resources are available on the Internet.

Of course, the things that promote health in your child also promote health in you. I urge you to monitor your own sleep, nutrition and overall lifestyle to see where you can provide better support for your mood and energy. Go to www.kidsandkaos.com and download my free e-booklet on improving the T.I.E.S. that Bind your Relationship. T.I.E.S. is an acronym for Time, Identity, Energy and Sex/Intimacy—the four areas that are hit hardest once you have children. The e-booklet provides useful tips on how to manage your time, retain your individual identity while in a relationship, recharge your energy, and improve your sex life.

CHAPTER 4

LAYING THE GROUNDWORK: Setting Limits and Expectations

The understanding you now have about why your child behaves as she does will help when you prepare to eliminate, reduce or encourage certain behaviors. Chapter 5 covers problematic behaviors you may want to eliminate or reduce, and Chapter 6 covers those you may want to encourage. In case you are tempted to jump ahead, first read the information on setting limits and expectations in this chapter since it will provide further groundwork for your preparation. This chapter only gives an overview of how to set limits and expectations. Later on you will be given plenty of detailed instruction, as well as illustrative examples, that will help you design your own limits and expectations to fit a variety of typical situations.

For each behavior you decide to help your child change, you will have to choose whether to set a limit, set an expectation, or both. As a general rule, set limits on those behaviors you want to reduce or eliminate, and set expectations on those behaviors you would like to start or increase. Use both limits and expectations when you want to substitute an undesirable behavior with a desired one.

Setting Limits

Perhaps the most important reason for setting limits is that it provides your child with the safe and predictable environment she needs, as discussed in Chapter 2. Such an environment gives her a sense of psychological safety and

69

a solid trust in the world around her. This, in turn, frees her from worry about things that should not concern her. Within clearly-defined limits and boundaries, she is free to focus her curiosity, intelligence and energy on doing what all children have a right to do: play, learn, grow, make mistakes, experience feelings, and have fun. In such an environment, she quickly learns if "A" happens, "B" follows, giving her a reassuring sense of predictability.

Provide an environment that is physically safe by childproofing your home or putting a gate around an outside play area or pool when she is young, making appropriate adjustments as she grows. The child within such safe boundaries can run and play without having to worry about where she can and cannot go. A good analogy of this is a boxing ring where, because of the physical boundary provided by the ropes, contestants do not need to keep their eyes on the perimeter of the raised floor. They know where the limits are by seeing and feeling the ropes. This allows them to conserve their vigilance and energy for the fight. The limits you set provide your child with the "ropes" she needs to be safe and keeps her focus where it belongs, on being a child.

For those of you who may be a little squeamish about setting limits on her behavior because you are not yet convinced that it is the right thing to do, please recall the discussion on leadership in Chapter 1. When you set limits, you are drawing a clear and necessary line in the sand and saying, in effect, "For your own good, you may not cross this line." When you hold firm to the limits you set, you are giving your child the message that you are serious about what you say. An important time to set limits is when she behaves in a threatening, aggressive or dangerous way. Such behaviors include verbal abuse, hitting, biting, kicking, spitting, running out of the house, or running away from you in public.

Standing your ground when those limits are tested is also essential. You can say, "Don't hit your brother again or I will put you in Time Out," but unless you actually follow through, setting that limit will not work.

I recently observed a situation that involved setting limits (or the lack thereof). At the time I found it amusing, although I am sure it was not amusing for the mother involved. With grown children I can now recall such episodes with a humor I didn't always have back when I was going through them myself!

I was in a grocery store on a weekday morning, typically a quiet time. I heard a loud, barely-restrained voice saying, "Jenny, don't touch the fruit. No, you can't put it in the buggy. Mommy will take you out to the car if you keep doing that." Not a moment later I heard the same voice saying, "Jenny, no, don't touch those. The man who put the groceries there won't like it." Another moment later, "Jenny, remember, we'll have to leave if you do that again." By now I was getting curious as to whether this harassed mom would hold the limit. About twenty minutes later, her voice was no longer quite so restrained and "Jenny" was now referred to by her entire name: "Jennifer Judith Smith, DO NOT touch the eggs or you will be in BIG trouble and I will have to take you to the car." Needless to say, Jennifer Judith was never taken to the car. Her behaviors continued unabated and mom's reactions became increasingly frazzled.

I describe this vignette not to humiliate all of us who have been there, but rather to illustrate how we cause (and how we can change) such behaviors. You will find many options on how to hold the limits you set in Chapter 7.

How to Set Limits

When setting limits, the first step in the process is the "setup" and the second is the "follow-through." The setup is crucial to having a successful outcome, so spend enough time on it to prepare yourself well.

The setup consists of selecting the behavior you would like to eliminate or change, deciding on which reinforcement technique you will use, and preparing the message you will deliver to your child *before* she engages again in the unwanted behavior. You can tweak what I suggest to fit your particular situation, but keep the following essentials in mind when doing so.

The Setup

- Make sure you and your partner agree on which behavior you want to eliminate and which technique you will use. To make life simple, choose just one behavior until you are satisfied with the outcome, then move on to the next.

- Select the technique you plan to use and review that section in the book to prepare yourself. Throughout the book as you read about a particular technique I suggest you use, refer to the Techniques Index on page 14 which will direct you to the page where you will find that suggested technique.

- Deliver the message to your child about which behavior you will no longer tolerate, why you will no longer tolerate it, and what will happen when she behaves that way again. Answer her questions until you are sure she fully understands the process, but do not get drawn into negotiating.

The Follow-through

- When she engages in the unwanted behavior, immediately remind her of your original message as you use the selected technique.

- Once you have followed through and held firm to the limit, move on to the rest of your day and help her do the same. Repeat this process until the behavior is eliminated. I suggest you not discuss her poor behavior immediately upon her release her from Time Out or whatever technique you selected. During the setup you told her why you wanted the behavior to stop, so she already knows the why of it.

Not all behaviors can be completely eliminated. For instance, it is unlikely you will ever completely eliminate sibling rivalry. Nor should you. The good news about sibling rivalry is that it actually provides a training ground for your children to learn the art of negotiation, fair play, compromise, and problem-solving. Eliminating it entirely would be counterproductive. All that is necessary is to reduce its annoying impact on you while your children learn the lessons it can provide.

Setting Expectations

As with setting limits, give your child a short, clear message about what you expect from her—and why—as the first step in making behavioral changes. Expectations differ from limits in that they are designed to encourage behaviors rather than to discourage or eliminate them. Techniques are provided in Chapter 7 to make sure the expectations you set are successful.

Knowing what is expected of her helps your child experience her environment as predictable and safe. It also gives her the opportunity to develop a sense of accomplishment and pride. If she does not know what to do (or what not to do), how can she know when she has accomplished the expected, and experience the resultant feelings of mastery and self-esteem? Between the age of five and eight she will increasingly provide her own internal methods of motivation and reward developed from her prior experience of effort and mastery, and rely less on external encouragement or reward from you. Until then, she still needs plenty of external encouragement and support.

How to Set Expectations

The process for setting expectations is similar to the process for setting limits, with its own setup and follow-through steps. The setup is easier than it is in setting limits, but the follow-through can be difficult because to enforce an expectation means you have less control over the outcome. Some of the techniques used to enforce expectations require you to take a step back, and wait to see what your child does with the expectation you have set. Parents who are fearful of relinquishing that control may feel threatened at first. But actually, when you take that leap of faith, you may experience the power of *being in control* for the first time. Some parents fear that letting go will signal they have given in and allowed their child to win. If you have set the expectation for the right reason, and follow through in the right way, your child will get the clear message that you are in charge. The techniques suggested in Chapter 7 are designed to work, and have proven to be successful over decades of use. All you have to do is set the stage, be patient, and let the technique do what it was designed to do.

Paradoxically, although failing to set expectations for your child can result in feelings of failure for her, you must be prepared to set an expectation and let her fail if she chooses not to comply with it. But because there is the potential for failure, you should set an expectation that cannot result in failure that is too disappointing for either of you. That will enable you to step back and comfortably give her room to succeed *or* fail.

The Setup

- Decide with your partner on one behavior you would like your child to start, or do more of.
- Select the reinforcement technique you plan to use. Throughout the book as you read about a particular technique I suggest you use, refer to the Techniques Index on page 14 which will direct

you to the page where you will find that suggested technique.

- If possible, attach the expectation to something she already enjoys, for example: "You can have your bath when you have picked up your toys." Saying it like this prevents it from sounding like a threat, as in "If you don't pick up your toys there will be no bath." Set expectations in a positive manner.

- When you are ready and she is in a receptive mood, simply let her know that from now on, you expect her to do (what you have decided) because you think she is big enough, old enough, or in some other way ready to do it. Tell her why you want her to engage in the behavior. You will be appealing to her natural enthusiasm and desire to accomplish a new skill—as well as her need to contribute.

- Make your voice positive and determined. Ask if she has any ideas of her own that she can use while preparing for or when performing the expected behavior. This strengthens the potential for follow-through since she is increasing her ownership of, and commitment to, the behavior with each idea she suggests.

Example: "I think you're old enough now to put your toys away at night right before your bath and it will help everyone keep the house tidy. Let's make sure you've got plenty of space to put everything away." Strategize with her how this will be done, using as much of her input as possible. You know she loves having a bath at night, so you can rely on that to provide her with motivation to tidy away the toys beforehand.

This is a good time to observe just how big a mess she might have to deal with. If you think the sheer number of toys she has to pick up will overwhelm her, clear away everything she rarely or never plays with and leave out only the toys she uses frequently.

The Follow-through

Once the set up is done, all you have to do is wait for her to pick up the toys—without a reminder. She may bring the subject up herself. If she does, be sure to engage with her fully in her discussions about tidying up, as your attention will greatly help. If she is very young, she may need a cue that it is almost bath time and time to pick up her toys. Remind her once only, then sit back and wait.

- **Outcome #1:** Your child tidies her toys. Do not expect perfection, but do expect to see effort and commitment to the task. Acknowledge it positively but don't go overboard. After all, she is doing what was agreed to, and should feel a sense of pride in her accomplishment. Most likely she will tell everyone who listens about her latest achievement and, as a result, will get additional praise. Follow up with the bath she enjoys and continue this until her behavior becomes habitual, giving it less attention as it becomes a habit.

- **Outcome #2:** She does not pick up her toys, or only picks up one or two things. Refrain from giving her a second reminder, but do not give her a bath either. Go through the rest of the evening as usual, making no mention of the toys or bath. She might not say anything about the toys, but she will probably say something about the missed bath. If she does bring it up, mention that you noticed her toys were still out, so there is no bath tonight. Let her know that she will have another chance tomorrow night. If she rushes to tidy up her toys and tells you it is bath time, stand firm and let her know she has missed the bath for tonight, but can try again tomorrow. Redirect her attention and spend the rest of the evening as you usually would.

- **Outcome #3:** Your child continues with Outcome #2 for a couple more nights. Now she is showing that she needs help to comply. Prepare her for, and implement the Bag technique.

Testing the Limits and Resisting Expectations

No chapter on setting limits and expectations would be complete without acknowledging the fact that it is normal for your child to test the limits and resist the expectations you set from time to time. Together, the limits and expectations you set comprise the boundaries of her environment and she is simply testing to see if those boundaries are as solid, predictable and safe as they seem. She needs to be sure that they will stay that way no matter what she does to push against them. She has to rely on the fact that if you say something, you mean it. If she tests the limit and it caves, or does not comply with an expectation and is allowed to get away with it, not only will her environment feel less secure, but she will be more resistant to changing her behavior the next time. You may even see an increase in her misbehavior as she continues to look for firm boundaries

Consider whining and other efforts to negotiate her way out of complying as annoying and unnecessary noise and ignore it.

CHAPTER 5

BEHAVIORS TO REDUCE OR ELIMINATE

Before I address the topic of reducing or eliminating unwanted behaviors, I want to impress upon you how important it is to recognize the impact of stress on your child's behaviors. It is fair to say that many behavioral problems (both yours and your child's) are stress related. In fact, this book is as much about reducing the level of stress in your home as it is about improving your parenting skills. If you follow the suggestions about how to do the latter, you will go a long way towards alleviating the former.

Do not forget that your child lives in the same pressured and stressful environment as you, but he has fewer coping skills with which to deal with the stress. He has to go to school, to sports, and to appointments as well as deal with the pressure of living in a world that holds him to high expectations. Where in all this activity is there time to relax, to just hang out with the family and recharge? It is in this pressure-cooker environment that he gets tired, yet must keep going and doing. He has to deal with you when you are hurried, harried, and have little patience with his dawdling and frustrating behaviors. Keep in mind that all of this contributes to the development of the behaviors addressed in the rest of this chapter.

For the sake of clarity, I have sorted a range of typical childhood misbehaviors into the following categories: Dangerous Behaviors, Aggressive Behaviors, "Water Torture" Behaviors, and Power Struggle Behaviors. A description of each of these is followed by a reference to the recommended technique that will help you manage or eliminate it. Refer to the Techniques

Index on page 14 for the page number for a particular technique. Remember to work with your partner so both of you can present a united front.

Many of the behaviors you encounter on a daily basis are merely frustrating, but they can become aggressive or dangerous if your child is:

- Left to misbehave without correction or given alternative choices about how to behave.
- Witness to the aggressive or dangerous behaviors of others.
- Exposed to neglect or abuse.

This chapter contains information on a range of dangerous and aggressive behaviors regardless of what has prompted them. Should certain behaviors place you and your child beyond the scope and help of this book, I advise that you seek professional help.

Dangerous Behaviors: Those That Threaten Physical and Psychological Safety

I classify dangerous behaviors as those your child performs, or is about to perform, that will put him or others in danger. Why might he do this? He may be too young to know his limits and does not realize he is putting himself or others in harm's way. He may be distracted and not notice the potential danger, or be copying what he sees the adults around him do. He may be emotionally overwhelmed by something and not thinking as he normally would, or he may have learned that certain behaviors get immediate attention. Whatever the reason, your swift response at such times is essential.

Although there are many potentially dangerous behaviors, the following seem to be at the top of the list for most parents:

- Running away or hiding in a crowded public place or just wandering off and getting separated from you.

- Dashing out from behind a car in a parking lot or in the street.
- Climbing or playing in an area where he is out of his element.
- Grabbing at or otherwise recklessly approaching a dog or other animal, whether or not he knows the animal.
- Running with or throwing sharp objects.
- Acting up in a car while it is in motion.
- Verbally, emotionally or physically abusing another person.

Make sure you and your partner agree on which behaviors are untenable. Tell him about the dangers—but only what he needs to know when he needs to know it—and teach him the rules that will keep him and others safe. For example, if he spends much time around swimming pools, make sure he knows and follows the safety rules that you feel are most critical.

Educate him over time as you think he is ready to learn and as exposure to certain dangerous situations becomes likely. For example, teach him the rules for staying with you in public places, what he should do when approached by strangers, how to approach animals, and how to call 911, etc. Keep the rules simple, clear, and specific. Successful management of dangerous behaviors lies as much in understanding and obeying the rules that prevent them as in using techniques to eliminate them. Test him regularly to see if he understands and remembers what rules you have taught him.

Once you are sure he knows what dangerous behaviors are and understands the rules, you can and should immediately address any infringement. Your swift and consistent response will convey a clear, unambiguous message about what he must not, or must, do. When addressing an infringement, you do not need to give him warnings or choices, because to do so could endanger him further. Simply use the selected reinforcement technique while explaining why you are using it, and make sure he understands. Some of the best techniques for dangerous behaviors are Time Out, The Quiet Place, Time Out in Public, Time out for a Toddler, and—when he has followed the rules and avoided the danger—Positive Reinforcement for following the rules you have taught him.

Running Away or Hiding in Public, Dashing Into a Street or Parking Lot, Playing In an Area Out of His Element, or Approaching an Unfamiliar Animal

Your child may not realize how serious a threat these behaviors pose for him, and although it may alarm you greatly when he engages in any of them, I urge you to stay calm. He may be scared when he realizes what he has done and your reaction will determine how well he calms down or how quickly he escalates. Remove him from danger as soon as you possibly can, make eye contact, and calmly but firmly tell him he cannot do that. Take him with you to a safe place such as the home or yard, the store, or the car. Remind him of the rules about such dangers, but reassure him he is safe, he made a mistake, and that you are not angry with him. I would not use a Time Out or similar technique for such infractions unless he is uncontrollably upset and needs to be contained. It is a good time however (once he has calmed down) to make sure he understands the rules and knows why and when to use them.

Acting Up in a Moving Car

Examples of behaviors in the car that come under this heading are thrashing about, kicking the back of the driver's seat, undoing the seatbelt, hurting others, throwing things around, and loud screaming. I mention this in the Dangerous Behaviors section because it can prove to be so distracting for the driver that it puts everyone in the car at risk. Use the Time Out in a Moving Car technique for this problem behavior.

Dangerous Behavior in a Toddler

I address both potentially dangerous and aggressive behaviors in a toddler in the section below under "Toddler Aggression."

Aggressive Behaviors: Those That Threaten Physical and Psychological Safety

There are many causes for aggressive behavior in young children. Here are just a few of the most likely:

- Your child's young age and immaturity may cause him to become overwhelmed by his emotions. He simply may not know how to adequately contain himself.
- He may not be getting as much physical activity as he needs and his pent-up energy is spilling over into impulsive or careless behavior.
- Perhaps he feels unfairly treated by another child and is retaliating.
- It could be that he knows aggressive behavior gets immediate attention from the adults around him.
- He may simply be copying other people who behave aggressively.

Aggressive behaviors must be stopped because they run the risk of becoming *dangerous* behaviors, as in when a child impulsively jumps on a dog that may bite him. It is also important to realize that even mildly aggressive behaviors can develop into seriously aggressive ones when a child is older, especially if his aggression is not addressed by providing him with correction early on or teaching him how to appropriately express himself. Like dangerous behaviors, aggressive behaviors must be dealt with immediately and effectively.

Serious Sibling Rivalry

Parents play a powerful role in determining how mild or how deadly their children's fights are. The behavior of one or both parents can cause serious sibling rivalry, and new behavior, based on a parent's educated intervention, can reverse it. The behaviors that characterize serious sibling fighting are different from the annoying behaviors observed in ordinary sibling rivalry. With serious fighting, one sibling can get badly hurt (physically, emotionally or psychologically), and it is usually the same sibling each time. These behaviors can be characterized as bullying inside the home. Here is how parents can unintentionally contribute to the problem:

- They take sides, pitting one child against the other, showing favoritism.
- They hold the same child responsible, or punish the same child every time, no matter who seems to be the perpetrator or the victim.
- They are physically, emotionally, or verbally abusive towards the children.
- Their own fights frequently become physically, emotionally or verbally threatening within view, or earshot, of the children.
- They demean the children.

Not only are parents modeling aggressive behavior, they are also building fear and resentment when they mismanage their children's fighting by taking sides and coming down harder on one child than another. Sooner or later, the fear and resentment among the children find an outlet in increasingly aggressive behaviors towards one other.

If you are concerned about your children's violent fighting, and the techniques you have tried are not working, seek professional advice from a coach on how to manage your own fighting behaviors. If you are reluctant to seek professional help yourself, consider getting it for your children, who may be afraid of your fighting, or resentful towards one another. Before implementing the technique suggested below, take time to carefully re-examine how your behaviors may be influencing your children, so that any techniques you use will be more effective.

The technique I suggest is Time Out for *each* child involved in the fight. Let them know ahead of time that Time Out will be the immediate consequence of a bruising physical or verbal altercation. Tell them why Time Out is necessary—that it is not a punishment, but rather a way to help them calm down and avoid getting hurt. Remember, the Time Out is for *both* (or all) of the combatants, not only the one who *seems* to be the aggressor. You will make things much worse if you take sides or only put the child who seems to be the aggressor in Time Out. Parents cannot referee because they do not know when, where, or by whom the fight was started. Time Out is *not* a punishment, merely a means to help your children cool off and contain themselves.

The swifter and more determined your response to serious sibling fighting, the quicker you will put an end to it. When your children complain about being in Time Out—because "it was his fault, not mine"—remind them that they are old enough to sort out their fights, but since they were not able to do it this time, they both (or all) have to cool off in Time Out.

For most behaviors that warrant a Time Out, I do not advocate immediately discussing the behaviors that got them there in the first place. Most of the time, the best thing to do is to move on and make no mention about what happened and let things settle back to normal. However, with serious fighting between siblings, some damage repair is needed to restore a sense of safety. Consider implementing some of the suggestions below.

Build their conflict-resolution skills. Once they have calmed down, engage them in brainstorming about alternative ways to settle their disputes. Elicit ideas from each of them. All input is valuable and should not be judged or ridiculed. Have each one identify one thing they will try differently the next time and make sure they follow through with their plan.

Commit to spending time alone with each child. Make it a priority to spend fifteen minutes each day with each child, reading or playing a game. Or commit to an hour each week, going for an ice cream, a trip to the park or library, or a walk with the dog. Whatever you decide to do, be consistent and persevere when it seems difficult to fit the time into your schedule. Just about anything else (except sleep) is less important than spending this critical time alone with him—even school activities or social commitments. If the problem is serious enough, time spent alone with him might even have to take priority over school and work. Although I'm not advocating skipping school or work on a regular basis, spending a mental health day, or half day, with him on a rare occasion will make time spent together so much more special for you both.

Put no conditions on time spent with each child. When you commit to spending time with him on a regular basis, do not attach any conditions. Do not withdraw this precious time for bad behavior or use it as a reward or motivation to behave well. He gets this time with you just because he is your child. Making such a time commitment while he is young will improve his behaviors and sense of self-esteem for life—and I am not exaggerating. During all my years as a psychotherapist, I never once heard an adult client say he had too much (or even enough) time with his parents when he was young. Not one client ever spoke about the money his parents made working long hours away from home, the wonderful homes they had or the expensive cars they drove. But I frequently heard clients recall spending quiet or alone time with one or both parents or doing something simple like baking, chatting, or congregating with other family members, and how good this felt. For some of them, such simple but profound memories brought tears to their eyes.

Develop family rituals so your children can feel proud about being part of a solid tradition. This can be as simple as sitting down together for dinner regularly (and refraining from rushing to an appointment halfway through). During those meals, give each person a chance to talk about his day or whatever else is on his mind. The Active Listening technique can make everyone's mealtime experience much richer. You can make the family ritual more elaborate by educating them about your ancestral culture, traditions and beliefs. Encourage them to do research and projects on their own. Help them develop pride and respect for their family and they will be less likely to trash it by fighting!

Enter your child's world. Allow your child to teach you about something he enjoys. Even if you know much more about the subject than he does, you can still learn something about him as you become his student. The importance he experiences from teaching you will give his self-esteem a big boost. Show sincere interest, and do not correct obvious mistakes or try to improve upon what he is teaching you. The goal of this exercise is not to increase his mastery of the subject matter, although that might happen. Instead, it is to give him evidence of your love with your undivided attention.

Beware the attention/fighting loop. It is likely that fighting between your children is due to a lack of attention, so if each child can experience you in the ways just described, the fighting will be reduced. Remember this rule of thumb: lack of attention results in fighting to get attention; fighting results in getting the wrong sort of attention; the right kind of attention reduces or eliminates the fighting.

Bullying

Bullying is another serious problem because it means that one person is physically, verbally and/or emotionally abusing another. Because of its potential severity, it frequently leads to the need for professional intervention.

I mention bullying in this chapter because it is an unfortunate reality in the lives of school-age children. However, the techniques described in this book may not be enough to help a bully make the necessary behavioral changes, develop the necessary social skills, or help his parents understand what they must change in their behaviors in order to support him. If that is the case, get professional help.

Although bullying can occur in the home (as discussed in the serious sibling rivalry section above), parents are more often made aware of their child's problematic behaviors by his teachers or school staff. They may not see the problematic behavior at home and, therefore, may not believe what they are hearing from school. However, if school personnel have notified you about your child's bullying, see it as an opportunity to help him, rather than being upset. Of course, you might have a strong reaction to the news and feel shocked, defensive, embarrassed, frustrated, or confused. All reactions are normal when you hear something unpleasant and disappointing about him. But make a concerted effort to put aside those feelings while you explore possible reasons for his alleged bullying behavior. Work hard with the school to find solutions to help him behave appropriately.

A bully is a child with low self-esteem who feels inadequate or insecure. Perhaps he has been ill-treated or has learned from watching other people that bullying is an acceptable way to behave. He usually picks on children who are defenseless, younger, smaller, shyer, or gentler than he is, and therefore are unlikely to retaliate. A bully sees such children as weak. Targeting and "conquering" them makes him feel stronger than he actually is.

The adults in a bully's life who are involved in helping him change his bullying behaviors—especially parents—must use effective corrective techniques, as well as find immediate ways to help him feel better about himself. If only his behavior is addressed, at best there will be a temporary change. If he is also helped to feel better about himself, any behavioral change he makes will be longer lasting. To help him, follow the suggestions outlined in the section above on Serious Sibling Rivalry, *as well* as getting help from a coach or counselor to develop better social skills.

If you know of a child who is on the receiving end of bullying behavior, be sure to bring it to the attention of an adult who can quickly provide him with the help he needs. The techniques in this book are not designed to provide such help alone.

Typical Sibling Rivalry

Typical sibling rivalry is designed for one purpose and for one purpose only: to get parents' attention. And it works! Just like whining and other annoying behaviors, parents can inadvertently cause sibling rivalry and, just as inadvertently, reinforce it. However, you will probably never eliminate the behavior entirely—nor should you. Handled well by parents, sibling rivalry can teach children how to negotiate and resolve conflict.

Not all sibling conflict is sibling rivalry. For example, if one of the siblings is too young to know what is going on or greatly mismatched in size and cannot handle it alone, that is not sibling rivalry and must be dealt with differently, as in the scenario below:

Example of exception to sibling rivalry: You have two sons, ages two and nine months. Your older son sees his younger brother crawling towards, and reaching for, one of his toys. He immediately rushes over and grabs it from the baby and knocks him aside, alarming him. The baby starts to wail. Your reaction will determine what happens next. If you are angry with your older son and blame him for upsetting the baby, you might increase the resentment towards his younger sibling, thus setting them up for sibling rivalry to develop later. Your two-year-old is actually behaving age-appropriately, so if you accept that, you will be more likely to react calmly and prevent the development of sibling rivalry between them.

What your two-year-old needs at a time like this is validation for being upset with the baby, a simple explanation about what happened, and an alternative choice for behaving in the future. Explain that you can see why he doesn't want the baby to take his toy, but the baby doesn't realize what he is doing, and did not mean to upset him. From there you can work out with him which of his toys the baby can play with, and leave it at that. Should he startle the baby again over taking a toy, he can be disciplined, since he has been told and has had time to learn and adjust to the new order of things. Discipline for an infraction of this sort at the age of two would simply be to take the offending toy away so that neither of them can play with it. Whenever he lets his younger brother use a toy, however, be sure to praise him for sharing. Do not expect him to share willingly yet. At two he is not able to understand such a complicated concept.

Typically, sibling rivalry occurs between siblings who are more closely matched in age, maturity, or size than the scenario I just described. How you handle it has as much influence on whether or not it continues, or gets worse.

Example of typical sibling rivalry: You hear your children—ages five and seven—bickering in another part of the house and you think, *here comes trouble.* Sure enough, a few moments later your five-year-old runs to you in tears because his older brother hit him or broke his toy. Perhaps you admonish the seven-year-old for picking on his younger brother, saying he should know better and tell him to apologize. Alternatively, it might be the seven-year-old who comes running in crying because his younger brother hurt *him.* This time you admonish the younger brother for what he allegedly did and tell *him* to apologize. While you are trying to sort it out, each child is out-shouting the other in an effort to convince you that they are the one who has been wronged and their brother should apologize and be punished.

If you do anything other than treat them both the same at this point, you will reinforce the behaviors you *don't* want, and ensure that resentment between them—and sibling rivalry—continues to thrive. If you don't believe their fighting constitutes serious sibling rivalry (as discussed earlier in this chapter), let them know you have every reason to believe that they can sort out their own fights and leave them to it. They will not do a perfect job the first time around, but if you consistently encourage them to sort out their own fights and praise them when they do, they will improve. You will also be helping them to develop important skills such as the ability to negotiate, collaborate, and resolve conflict.

Even if you are *convinced* you know who is to blame, you can never know for sure. Taking sides will only make one feel resentful and the other feel guilty. Also, remember that most sibling rivalry is designed to get your attention, so don't support it. There are many healthier ways for them to get the attention they need. When they have annoying fights like this, it is best to give them the benefit of the doubt and convey your confidence that they can sort it out. Use the Active Ignoring technique for all kinds of typical sibling fights; use a stronger technique such as Time Out or the Quiet Place when things have escalated beyond annoying.

When you decide to influence change in your children's fighting, give them a heads up (unless you are dealing with dangerous or aggressive behaviors, in which case, deal with it as described in the section on Dangerous Behaviors in this chapter). *Before* they get into a fight again—ideally when they are being friendly with each other—tell them you are pretty sure they can resolve their fights without your help and they should not expect you to do it for them any longer. Tell them that when they fight you will ignore it, knowing that they are taking care of it themselves. They will test you at first, perhaps by keeping the fight going, or by fighting a little more seriously, but stand firm and the fight will most probably fizzle out for lack of attention.

Always have a predetermined point at which you will step in and separate the combatants if things get out of hand. If you need to step in, use the Time Out technique.

When I first decided to ignore the sibling rivalry between my youngest two daughters (ages three and five at the time), I was concerned that they would hurt one another. Fortunately, they did not. After telling them that I would ignore future fights, and let them sort them out, I waited only a short time until the next fight. They fought for a while and gave up when I continued to ignore them. The second time I ignored their fighting, my three-year-old actually said, "Oh, there's no point, she won't take any notice." Then they went off and played. I was completely floored and wanted to tell the world what a great parent I was. Whenever they fell back into fighting again, I knew it was because I had been sucked in and my meddling was feeding the behavior. All I had to do was ignore it in order to stop it. I have seen this approach work with many, many parents, but it takes a certain amount of determination to try it.

Below I have categorized a number of other aggressive behaviors into two groups, based on the level of aggression usually manifested with each. Because sibling rivalry is uniquely connected to the relationship between parents and children, it warranted its own section. Just know that the following behaviors may happen with—or apart from—sibling rivalry as well.

Toddler Aggression

Although you may think a child under the age of two and a half is too young to engage in dangerous or aggressive behaviors, their immaturity and inability to adequately express themselves verbally, can in fact pose a danger to them or unintended aggression towards others. The greatest danger they pose to themselves is in doing such things as running into the street, running away from you in public and getting lost, falling into a swimming pool, and so on. Unintended aggression, or letting off steam from frustration at not being able to make themselves understood, can be seen in such behaviors as biting, hitting, or scratching others, or even hurting themselves in the same way. Don't be alarmed that any of these behaviors indicate your child is showing early signs of delinquency; he knows of no alternative ways of dealing with his world and needs firm and gentle guidance from you to handle things more effectively. Most young children will, on rare occasions, hit or bite, but if such behavior becomes more intense, frequent or prolonged, then you must step in and help your child stop.

Using Time Out in the usual sense on a child under the age of two and a half does not usually work well. He needs to be shown a clear and simple connection between his immature behavior and your response. I suggest using Time Out with a Toddler.

Group 1 (Serious) Behaviors

Group 1 behaviors are not behaviors children should habitually engage in as they include biting, spitting, kicking, punching, hair-pulling, grabbing at the body, and excessive teasing. Many of these behaviors are also seen in serious sibling rivalry. They differ here in that they occur between children who are not necessarily related, and all sides are involved in the fight. As with all aggressive behaviors, the first thing to do when dealing with Group 1 behaviors is to evaluate just how serious the situation is. Are the children involved drawing blood or giving one another a physical or emotional bruising? Do the fights occur each time friends come over or a group gets together? Do certain children seem to be more aggressive—or aggressive more often—than the others? Have you been trying to get it to stop for weeks or months? If you answered "yes" to any of these questions, then it is indeed a serious situation that needs immediate attention and relief. Do the fights only occur on rare occasions? Do the children involved only sometimes respond to your efforts to stop them? If you answered "yes" to these questions, you still need to intervene.

Group 1 behaviors indicate angry or fearful feelings in the children who engage in them. They are not normal childhood behaviors and all the children involved need help to resolve the issues and learn alternative ways of behaving. Not only could it be frightening for those involved, but also for those children who witness others behaving in this way, since they might feel threatened and unsafe. You must restore a sense of safety to the environment.

There is no need to prepare the children with any kind of warning. Instead, when you see one of them engage in a Group 1 behavior, stop whatever you are doing and tell them firmly (but not angrily) that you do not, and will not, allow that behavior to go on. Immediately separate them to their own Time Out or Quiet Place areas and follow through with determination. Show no favoritism since that might make the aggressive behaviors continue and, perhaps, get worse. Group 1 behaviors cannot be ignored because the situation could suddenly become dangerous if not addressed.

For all these behaviors, I advocate discussion with the children (after the fight and when they have calmed down) about how to express strong emotion and deal with conflict. Get them to brainstorm alternative ways of behaving. Make the assumption that feelings have been hurt, even if nobody is willing to admit it, and have each child involved in the fight think of something positive he can do for the group to help repair ill feeling. If something has been broken during a fight, be sure that *each* of the children involved makes restitution by working to pay for repairing or replacing what was broken. You do not need to come up with all the ideas; you can leave that to their imaginations. Then make sure they follow through.

Group 2 (Less Serious) Behaviors

These include shoving, horseplay, "Pig Pile," or grabbing at toys or clothes. Group 2 behaviors are rough play, with children laughing, giggling, and, in general, just horsing around. Such behaviors do not usually escalate to anything more serious. But always keep in mind that they *could*, and be ready to step up your response as necessary. If you are comfortable that they are just playing, even though it is rough and nobody is getting hurt, then you should leave them to it. If they begin to get serious, one of them will let you know and then you can step in if necessary.

Children may just be engaging in Group 2 behaviors to get your attention. If that attention is not forthcoming, they will soon give up unless they know you will "cave" when they turn up the heat. If you intervene too soon—while they are just playing—you could actually make them behave more aggressively as you take sides or give them the impression they were misbehaving. The most effective approach is to use the Active Ignoring technique.

"Water Torture" Behaviors

I call these typical attention-seeking behaviors water torture behaviors because it brings to mind the Chinese water torture technique in which a victim is subjected to hours of water being dripped, one drop at a time, on the forehead. As innocuous as one drop of water can be, almost imperceptible in fact, the practice was said to cause insanity. Whether mythical or real, it is an apt metaphor for what parents experience from behaviors such as whining, bossiness, bickering, interrupting, tattling, sulking, and pouting, dawdling, tantrums, screeching and screaming. And, just as water torture was designed to get the prisoner's attention and compel him to give up information, each of your child's water torture behaviors are designed for the same purpose—to get your attention and compel you to give them your time!

As well as being attention-seeking, water torture behaviors often indicate that your child is feeling insecure and is looking for a sturdy boundary, one that won't cave. Enabling him in some way to stop behaving poorly restores the sense of safety and predictability he is seeking and reduces his use of water torture behaviors.

In and of themselves, water torture behaviors are not dangerous or aggressive. But they have, at times, resulted in some children's lives being put in danger at the hands of overwhelmed and inexperienced caregivers, so it is best to prevent the habit from developing, or break it when it has. Most of the time, however, water torture behaviors just prove to be highly annoying and do not put anybody in real danger. The technique I recommend to eliminate most water torture behaviors is Active Ignoring, which is easy to learn and gets immediate results.

Whining

Whining is probably first on your list of "A Parent's Top Ten Woes" and one I am asked to address everywhere I go. Whining, like sibling rivalry, is a great example of how you can cause poor behavior without any awareness of having done so. Let me illustrate what I mean.

Step one of the Whining Dance probably catches you with your guard down. One day your child asks for something in his normal non-whiny way. However, you are focused on something that has your complete attention (an emergency, a migraine, a phone call, etc.) You do not hear him, so you do not answer him as he expects. Perhaps he patiently repeats his request, with the same non-response from you. Finally, he turns up the volume, alters the pitch of his voice, and manages to get through your mental fog. Now you hear him! But his tone and volume annoy you; it is not his normal sound at all. You notice this and react by giving him your negative attention. By doing this you have now taught him that whining results in a response from you.

From this point forward, whenever he wants you to pay attention, and your response is not quick enough, all he has to do is whine.

Step two of the Whining Dance begins when you want him to stop. You ask him to use his normal voice. You tell him he cannot have what he is asking for until he stops whining. You tell him no, no, no, a hundred times. You call him by his full name and tell him to stop. You threaten: "Santa doesn't bring present to kids that whine." You bribe: "I'll take you for ice cream if you stop whining." And he keeps on whining. Get the picture? We've all been there! That is how it starts. Would you like to know how to stop it?

Ignore it!

You read that correctly. Completely ignore it by using the Active Ignoring technique. Let him know what you plan to do, and why, then when he whines, simply do nothing. Be deaf. Tune him out. Occupy yourself with something that keeps you from giving him any attention, including eye contact. He will eventually stop and give up if you consistently ignore him. If he cranks up the volume, let him crank. If you are in public and want to avoid embarrassing him or yourself, use Time Out in Public. Be warned, this new response—or rather non-response—from you may escalate his behavior until he needs a different method to calm himself down. In that case, I suggest The Quiet Place technique. When he has stopped whining and complaining about being disciplined, act as normal. Make no reference to, or engage in any discussion of, his whining behavior, since you told him what you were going to do, and why. Be sure to attend to him promptly when he asks you for something in his normal way to reinforce the behavior you want. There is no need to give him everything he asks for, but do respond. Once you have mastered the Active Ignoring technique, you have control over whether or not the whining continues.

Bossiness

First children, only children, or children born with naturally strong personalities tend to be bossy more often than other children, but this is not always the case. Bossiness can be a sign of insecurity, it can be a misguided attempt to join or lead a group of playmates, or simply a habit picked up from seeing bossiness in others. Rarely does the behavior become aggressive, although occasionally a bossy child will retaliate against those who ostracize him. Bossiness can provoke aggression or unkind treatment from other children and a bossy child can end up a lonely child.

If others are concerned that your child is bossy, you may be unconcerned because you misinterpret his behavior as self-confidence. You may have even contributed to his habit if you thought this trait was cute when he was a toddler and encouraged it by your reaction. Sometimes a young child's natural ebullience can make him seem bossy. If you get feedback from others that your child's "self-confidence" is more than that, take it seriously and help him understand the impact of his behavior on others. He may be totally unaware that there is any connection between his behavior and the response he gets. He might be glad to know there is something he can do to be more popular. Help him develop alternative ways of behaving.

When your child is being bossy with you, do not fuel the behavior with any reaction (either negative or positive), and do not give in to his demanding ways. Tell him you will not respond when he orders you around, and when you see him bossing others, step in and model the appropriate behavior.

Example: One child to another child as he grabs a ball: "Give me the ball and I'll show all of you how to do it. You guys go over there, you guys go over there, and I'll stay here and be coach." If the other children follow his orders, it will not be for long as they drift off to play something more enjoyable, something not being led by a pint-sized sergeant major. Step in, take the ball from the "coach" and ask the whole group what they would like to do.

Then heed their requests. Do not do anything that would shame the coach, and either take over the role of coach yourself, or hand it over to another child, so that the coach becomes just one of the group. Ignore his protests and let him choose to join in or remove himself from the group.

Bickering

Bickering can be every bit as annoying as whining, but since more than one child is involved, bickering can do more damage to your ears and sanity—and do it more quickly—than whining. If it is your children doing the bickering, it can hurt you to observe two people you love behaving this way with one another. Do not give in to the temptation to play referee, or preach to them about why they should not argue with one another but again, simply ignore it. As with whining, you might be the cause, but not necessarily so. All it takes is for one child to do something that provokes the other and they are off to the races without your help. There is a reason I suggest you avoid playing referee and ignore the bickering: it is actually none of your business. It is the business of the children involved.

I can hear you say, "What if one of them asks me to sort it out, or what if I can clearly see that one is treating the other unfairly or unkindly?" I still urge you to resist the temptation and leave the responsibility for sorting it out to the children. If you must intervene, get them to think of other ways to resolve the disagreement. The benefit of this approach is that they will learn an important skill (conflict resolution) of which they can feel proud. Furthermore, if they were bickering in the first place solely to get your attention, they will stop once you pay their behavior no attention. Reinforce any positive move they make towards resolution by acknowledging and praising their efforts.

If they resent being ignored by you and up the ante in an attempt to drag you in, their bickering may go from verbal to physical or get louder and louder. If all else fails, they may resort to name-calling, swearing, or engaging in some other behavior that has previously brought you into the fray. Continue to ignore it or it will continue unabated. If the physical fighting gets more bothersome and cannot be ignored, separate them and put them *both*—or all—in Time Out or Quiet Place.

Interrupting

Although it sometimes seems as if children are born with the ability to interrupt, this is yet another behavior you may have inadvertently started, but also have the ability to stop. Interrupting can pack a powerful punch because it is often used in combination with whining.

Here is how the habit can begin: You are talking on the telephone to a friend. Without thinking, you turn to your child when you feel his tap on your leg and ask him what he wants. He tells you. You may or may not immediately interrupt your conversation for him, but he now knows that when he taps your leg he can draw your attention away from what you are doing and get you to focus on him. He taps again and his interrupting begins to annoy you and you say with irritation, "Wait until I've finished my conversation." Does he wait? No, a few moments later the tapping starts again! Now you snap at him to be patient. Finally you end the conversation and turn on him irritably as you say, "Leave me alone when I'm talking on the phone!"

Newsflash: his interrupting will not stop until you use Active Ignoring because any reaction from you constitutes attention and reinforces his interrupting. Tell your friend that you are going to ignore any interruptions from him during your conversation, which may be distracting. When he taps your leg, continue talking. Talk about anything that comes into your head, but resist responding to the tapping. Keep the conversation going until the tapping has stopped, and then end your conversation. As soon as you have hung up the phone, thank him for not interrupting. Then ask him what it is he wants from you. He actually may have forgotten.

Being interrupted by one child is tough enough, but when you are frequently interrupted by several children at once, life can become unbearable. To avoid this, get a handle on any interrupting behaviors early on.

Your child may be in the habit of interrupting his friends, too. You can try talking to him about why he should not do this, but if the other children do not seem to mind or notice his interruptions and just continue with what they are doing, do not make a big deal out of it. Children often butt in on one another's conversations and usually socialize each other out of the habit. However, if you can see that his interrupting is bothering his friends to the extent that they have begun to exclude him from their play, you will need to help him make the connection between his interrupting behavior and their reactions.

Tattling

Every parent seems to have their least loved water torture behavior and this one was mine. When my children tattled on one another, I tended to show the basest part of my personality. Tattling probably stems from your child's feeling that he has been misunderstood, or unfairly blamed for something, and that someone else should actually get the blame. Tattling may be used as payback; a way to even the score with another child. Sometimes your child may think he can earn brownie points with you if he shows how good he is by tattling on someone else. Whatever the real cause of the tattling, you—and probably he—will never know for sure. It is often what goes on with typical sibling rivalry and the way to manage it is the same: Active Ignoring. However, if you have not already done so, have a conversation with your child about why you do not want him to tell tales and make the distinction for him between what you mean by telling tales as opposed to letting you know something you should know.

Because you cannot know for sure what the real truth is when your child tattles to you, refrain from playing referee. Even if you think you know what the truth is, do not take sides because it can cause resentment between the children, and between them and you. Let them try to solve the problem.

Example: You see Matt hit Sam and Sam tattles on Matt. How do you know what they were doing to each other before Matt hit Sam? You can never know, and you can never win. What you can do is ask how they might work it out or assure them they are well able to sort it out themselves. They will either forget all about it or they will learn more about how to play fair and resolve conflict. There is nothing to lose if you stay out of it, but plenty to lose if you jump in. If for some reason you must get involved, do so without judgment and without focusing on the tattling.

Example: Matt runs in to tell you Sam is doing something he is not allowed to do and in the process has cut his leg and is bleeding. Attend to the bleeding leg, but do not get into a lecture on why they should not tell tales on one another.

Sulking, Pouting and Dawdling

There may be times when your child seems sulky and resistant to joining a social activity, and you may never know the cause. This usually happens during a family outing, while on vacation, or when you are otherwise trying to enjoy a memorable event. Often when you ask what's wrong, he says, "Nothing." Or you may get a reply that makes little sense. My guess is that a change in the routine or an increase in the tempo of activity may be overwhelming to the point of stimulus overload. All he may need is to relax quietly until he feels ready to join in again. Alternatively, he may have learned that he gets more attention if he behaves this way.

The rest of the family need not suffer and should be allowed to fully enjoy whatever is going on, so it is best to downplay this type of behavior.

Trying to get him to join in and behave in a happy, positive manner is too much to expect. Getting upset with him will not be productive either, and it could make things worse. If he does need to get away from the hustle and bustle of activity, help him do that. Obviously he cannot be left alone in an amusement park or at the beach while everyone else enjoys the festivities, so an adult will have to stay with him. If possible, see to it that whoever stays remains calm and uncritical. He will snap out of it when he is ready or will get back home, sleep a sound sleep, and wake up refreshed. If it is not convenient or possible to have an adult stay with him, just let him be quiet and sulky with the family. At least he is safe. If he derives no benefit from ostracizing himself, he will soon join in. When he does decide to join in, carry on as normal and include him, without comment, in whatever activity is going on.

The occasional grumpy day should not be cause for alarm and you do not need to be worried about depression unless there is probable cause, such as a recent loss or significant disappointment, or if his sulkiness lasts for weeks at a time. If you are concerned about depression, monitor his moods, and take note of any changes in sleep, appetite and concentration, (all of which are signs of depression) for a week or two. Then bring your observations and concerns to the attention of his pediatrician.

Dawdling and other foot-dragging behaviors usually occur when the family is rushed for time, such as getting ready for school and work. Sleepy-heads, both children and adults, are required to get up, brush teeth, dress, gather together items needed for the day, eat breakfast, and pack lunch. This makes it hard to concentrate and difficult to accomplish everything in a timely manner. So first consider whether everyone is getting enough sleep. Getting your child up a little earlier, suggesting he prepare the night before, or just giving him less to do during those busy times will also help. After doing all you can to help him, do not pester or nag. Let him do the best he can while you tend to your own activities. Chapter 8 covers how to establish family routines, and it might be helpful to read it if your morning time is being disrupted by dawdling or crankiness.

Tantrums, Screeching and Screaming

Your child will most likely collapse into a rage at some point in the form of out-of-control screaming or tantrums. The difference between the two is that although a tantrum certainly can involve screaming, it also includes some sort of physical performance such as kicking. Your child may throw himself on the ground, bang his head or feet on something, or hit himself or someone else. Don't be alarmed by this type of behavior, even though it can look and sound quite violent. Of course, if he is banging his head, hitting something dangerously hard, or hurting somebody, he will have to be contained by a Time Out or taking him to the Quiet Place. Most tantrums and screaming fits are usually brought on by a build-up of frustration that overwhelms his ability to emotionally contain himself, and will happen less frequently as he matures. By the age of five or six, they should be a thing of the past. If not, examine your reactions; you may be fuelling them without realizing it.

Observe his tantrums. Identify what starts him off so you can be alert for the signs and redirect him earlier in the process, thereby preventing such overwhelming frustration. Is he more likely to have a meltdown when tired or hungry? During transitional times? At specific times of the day? Sometimes he might go from normal behavior to full-blown tantrum in a matter of seconds, but usually you can see the progression and figure out a way to calm him down before he gets to the meltdown point. Other than prevention, the best approach, once a tantrum or screaming fit is under way, is to use the Active Ignoring or the Quiet Place techniques. I would suggest you not try to head off tantrums by making promises or he will use them as a means to get what he wants in the future. Threats will not head it off either, so the best you can do is manage them as suggested above.

Power Struggle Behaviors

A power struggle is an interaction between two (or more) people who are defending their territory, an opinion, an idea or a request. As each clings to his position, he rapidly comes to see the other as an opponent. As a result, a stalemate develops in which neither side succeeds in convincing the other to alter his thoughts or actions. Strangely, a kind of banging-your-head phenomenon then takes hold. Each opponent increasingly steps up his efforts to change the other's mind by using the same approach, even though it is not working. Feelings of competition then get stirred up, increasing each person's determination not to give in.

You know you are engaged in a power struggle when you find yourself blowing a lot of hot air, nagging, and otherwise having futile, unproductive and frustrating exchanges. No matter how many times you ask your child to do—or not do—something, nothing changes. Say you have repeatedly asked him to bring his bike into the garage at night. You have encouraged him, done it with or for him, threatened to take away privileges, and taken away privileges. He still does not bring in the bike. Ultimately, you throw your hands up in defeat and the bike stays outside.

There are several possible causes of a power struggle like this. First, the lack of parent training results in many of us feeling less than confident that we are doing the right thing for our children by disciplining them; we second-guess ourselves when we discipline, especially when they challenge our approach. Our hesitation makes it hard to stand firm, and leaves us vulnerable to—and drawn into—power struggles. A second cause could be your child's unconscious attempt to make you take control and set some limits. A third possible cause is simply that power struggle behaviors have become a habitual way of communication.

A power struggle is easy to get into and it feels like a maddening tug-of-war. You reprimand your child for something and he says, "No, I didn't!" and you reply, "Yes you did!" Or you ask him to do something and he says, "No, I won't." Waiting or hoping for him to withdraw or comply with you is unrealistic, since he does not fully realize the impact of his behavior. Again, you have inadvertently engaged in and nurtured a power struggle. One of the best ways to settle the stalemate is to withdraw from the fight. It may then be possible to reach a compromise once the power struggle is over.

Power struggles are exhausting and infuriating because you end up doing more work, fretting, and worrying than your child ever does. You are the one invested in his doing, or not doing, something—but he does not seem particularly invested at all. Your wasted effort is what ultimately exhausts and infuriates you. The good news is that when you withdraw from a power struggle, you end up putting the responsibility and the sweat and blood effort where it belongs: with your child. Let him know that in the future you plan to back out of arguments that go nowhere and let him do the important work of deciding how to proceed. He will learn something from the consequences that occur as a result of his decision. If your withdrawal does nothing else, it improves your relationship with him and encourages the development of his decision-making skills. When I suggest that you withdraw from a power struggle, let me calm any fears you may have that your withdrawal indicates he has gained an unhealthy upper hand. A sailboat metaphor I sometimes use helps to illustrate the necessity to withdraw:

By being taut and firm, sails provide a sailboat with the means of purposeful movement as they resist the prevailing winds. Without any wind, the sails are useless and the boat remains relatively still, moved along without purpose by the water. Imagine your child as the sails, and you as the wind that he can resist. If you remove your wind from his sails, he can no longer resist you and is left to provide propulsion from his own motivation, desire, or decision to comply with your requests. He then has the opportunity to learn how to behave autonomously and independently—and *respond* to his own internal messages—rather than behaving dependently and *reacting* to yours.

By withdrawing from the fight, you are actually teaching him some valuable lessons, which is an important part of parenting. When he is young, he needs your help to learn age-appropriate behaviors. Every time he misbehaves, he gives you an opportunity to guide him in the right direction. You are there to provide him with the necessary external motivation and reward to get it right. As he learns how to behave with your help, he develops his own internal guidance system and means of propulsion, motivation, and reward that will eventually allow him to manage his own behavior. Teaching him how to behave is an enormous responsibility for you, but it is also a tremendous gift for him—the gift that keeps on giving.

Not Listening, Cooperating or Complying

I wonder how many times you have asked yourself (or somebody else) in exasperation, "Why doesn't my child *listen* to me or do what I ask? He's so stubborn and it makes me mad!" Don't worry. This is a common frustration, and you are not alone. Getting through to him can be difficult, as it can be with anyone in your life. Start by asking yourself why you might tune somebody out. Perhaps they are boring or annoying, you may be tired or too busy to listen, you may hear them, but have no idea what they're talking about, or you perceive them to be a nag. Perhaps you choose not to listen or respond because they do not listen or respond to you. There are many reasons you may tune somebody out, and just as many reasons why your child may tune you out.

Your frustration may be due to the fact that he seems to be actively disengaging from the power struggle, but passively being a part of it. What you are experiencing when this happens is an example of passive-aggression. His non-expressed anger is expressed instead in passive or resistant behavior, which results in *you* feeling the anger he should be feeling or expressing. He may behave in a passively-aggressive way because to be actively or outwardly angry or aggressive would get him into trouble or result in him losing the fight. Or he may simply be unaware of either his anger or the reaction it evokes in you.

When he seems to be stubbornly refusing to comply with your request, you may feel disempowered—certainly you will feel frustrated and possibly perplexed. You may have given him several choices, (none of which he's taken you up on), tried a bribe or two, or a few gentle (or not so gentle!) threats. Still—nothing. What is left? First, you can ask yourself what his resistant behavior is telling you. He may be focused on something more interesting to him, or he could really be resisting what you are asking or telling him to do because he does not know how, or does not want to do it. Whatever the cause, you must take the lead and step out of the power struggle. I do not mean that you simply walk away and ignore him, but that you change your tactics so you can influence a change in his behavior.

If you think his focus is on something more interesting he might need a little time to refocus, so patiently repeat your request after a few moments. If you suspect he is resisting because he does not understand what you want, ask if he understands you, then listen to his answer, even if you do not agree with it or think he is not serious. At some level, he is bound to be wondering what is in it for him. Try to work it out with him using Active Listening. If that does not work, you could set a consequence:

Example: "Jake, I asked you to take out the trash before dinner. I've asked you five times since you got home and you still haven't done it. What's going on?"

"I'm busy."

"Doing what?"

"Watching my movie. I'll do the trash when it's over."

You could go over to the television and turn off the movie but that will only start another fruitless exchange. Set a consequence by telling him, "Okay, you can have dinner when you've taken the trash out. We'll be eating in ten minutes."

Outcome #1: Your child takes out the trash and joins you at dinner. Acknowledge him for following through.

Outcome #2: Your child comes to the table without having put the trash out and sees no plate at his place. He complains and starts to sit down. You remind him that he can have dinner when he has put out the trash, but that dinner will be over in fifteen minutes. He takes out the trash before dinner is over, you thank him, and he eats with you.

Outcome #3: He does not take out the trash and comes to the table when dinner is over. You remind him that he can have another chance to take out the trash in time for dinner tomorrow night. Keep this up until he complies. Do not substitute dinner with snacks later on, since it was his choice to skip dinner by not taking out the trash.

Defiance

Defiance is not a passive power struggle behavior—it is definitely an active one. When your child defies you, he either refuses to obey by telling you so, or he disobeys by doing the opposite of what was asked. Although it may not seem this way when it happens, rarely is a child defiant just for the heck of it, so it pays to discover what is causing his behavior.

Perhaps he is defiant because you are imposing your request on him without clearly explaining why, or you are failing to get enough buy-in from him. Alternatively, he may know that he is unable to do what is asked and is afraid or embarrassed to let you know. Perhaps he is angry with you and this is one way he can show it. Maybe, from his perspective, you are acting defiantly towards him. So take a close look at how you are handling the situation, before you decide how to proceed.

Once you have eliminated any behaviors of yours that may be contributing to the situation, the best way to find out why he is being defiant is to ask him, using Active Listening. Helping you understand will depend on his ability to articulate his thoughts and feelings, and his level of trust in you. If that does not work, choose Withdrawing from the Fight, or Setting a Natural or Created consequence.

Example: "Josh, it's time to get ready for school now. We're leaving in a minute."

"No! I can't stand school and I'm not going today!"

Instead of engaging in an argument when he is in such a defiant mood, choose one of the following options:

- Validate him by responding in a casual but no-nonsense voice that you know he doesn't like school some days, but that he has to go anyway. Help him get his things ready and walk him out to the car or bus stop. If he usually takes the bus but misses it that day, drive him to school, and if he is late, let him experience whatever consequences the school applies for late arrivals.
- Try to determine why school is bothering him by using the Active Listening technique to see if there is something you need to bring to the school's attention. Then tell him what you will do to help.

Whichever option you choose, he ends up going to school and receives the clear message that attending school isn't negotiable, but that you will help him sort out any legitimate problems.

KIDS & KAOS: Restoring Calm through Behavioral Change

Arguing

Arguing is an active behavior that combines elements of negotiating and defiance, and is a textbook example of a power struggle. The exchange can vary from annoying to enraging. As suggested in the preceding section on defiance, ask yourself how your behavior might be contributing to the exchange. It can be hard to be your own judge and observe that you are part of the problem in an argument, but logic dictates that there has to be more than one person for an argument to occur, and you are the other person in this case.

Are you trying to show your authority by having the last word? Are you talking *at* him instead of *with* him? Are you shouting or talking over his attempts to speak? Do you interpret his attempts to make himself heard as showing disrespect towards you? If that is the case, you are probably feeling irritated or insulted, and could be losing your perspective. I am not suggesting that you are totally accountable for the argument, but your involvement certainly fuels it. One thing you can do is simply withdraw, let your child know that is what you are doing, and why (because it gets you both nowhere), and focus on something else.

Example: Jack has grabbed a book out of his younger brother Joe's hand, just as you were about to sit down and read it with him. Your request that he return the book to Joe is met with a defiant "No, I want to read it." You quickly assess that trying to discuss the matter with Jack will stretch into a marathon event, so you decide to end it as soon as you can. Tell Jack that you do not allow grabbing, ask him one last time to give you the book, thank him and return it to Joe if he complies. If Jack runs off with the book, let him go. If he stands there and refuses to return the book, simply ignore him. In both cases turn your attention to Joe, and read a different book with him. Jack will soon feel the pinch of being left out when he sees you giving your attention to his brother. If arguing with you or not returning the book means that his brother gets your attention and he is left out, the arguing will soon stop. At any time he returns the book, remember to thank him. You have just modeled for him that arguing with you results in no attention, but complying gets positive attention.

Negotiating

Negotiating is highly annoying because it combines the best (or worst!) elements of whining, arguing and defiance. In a professional situation, the ability to negotiate can be an asset. However, negotiating with a three- or seven-year-old is not! You know you are mired in negotiation when your child tries to push one deal on you after another. The net result is that your initial request is overlooked in the verbal turmoil. The more you relent, the more he pushes and backs you into a corner. Constant negotiating can leave you feeling frustrated, whereas non-manipulative negotiation which results in either a valid compromise or a win for both parties, leaves you both feeling satisfied. Some children habitually use negotiating as a way to get what they want, or avoid something they don't want. Allowing your child to become a negotiator does him no favors because his friends and other adults will not warm to such behavior.

If he negotiates with you frequently, it is probably because you have unwittingly trained him to do so by giving him too many choices, giving choices before he is old enough to handle them, or making deals with (bribing) him. In all these cases, you are teaching him, by modeling, how to manipulate by negotiation. You can also create a negotiator by failing to hold firm to the limits or expectations you set. He quickly realizes there is plenty of wiggle room when you ask something of him and he seizes the opportunity to argue his point so that he can do what he wants instead of what *you* want.

Fortunately you can guide him into dropping this annoying habit before it is too entrenched by Withdrawing from the Fight, Setting an Expectation, or using a Natural or Created consequence. Acknowledge any progress with Positive Reinforcement and allow him express his frustration while you use Active Listening. Resort to the Quiet Place technique if he becomes over-wrought and needs help to contain his emotions.

Example: "Sam, it's almost dinnertime – time for piano practice."

"How about I take my shower now, have dinner, then practice?"

"That won't leave you enough time to get ready for bed."

"Then I'll eat dinner quickly and make time."

Well, you know how long that kind of back-and-forth can go on, and piano practice gets overlooked. What can you do? First, find out if he really wants to continue playing the piano. Is it what he wants, or what *you* want? If he really does not enjoy the piano, it is probably best to let him drop it. He can always take it up when he is older, with a different set of expectations. Constant fighting over the issue is likely to put him off playing anyway. On the other hand, if he wants to continue with piano lessons, you will need to get some buy-in from him, set a consequence, and even then, be prepared to stop the lessons if necessary.

Example (getting buy-in): "I've decided not to fight any more about you doing your piano practice, but first I have a couple of questions. Do you want to continue with it?"

"Yes." (If he says "no," make sure that ending the lessons is really what he wants.)

"How often does your teacher say you need to practice?"

"Three times a week."

"Good. So tell me which days you want to practice, how long, and when?"

"Monday, Tuesday and Thursday for twenty minutes before dinner."

"Great! You came up with a good plan. How are you going to re-member it?"

"I'll put it on my white board."

"Sounds like that'll work. Good job!"

Example (setting a consequence): "But if you don't follow your plan for some reason, I'll assume you no longer want to play, and I'll let your teacher know that we won't be coming for any more lessons. That way we're not wasting everyone's time and money."

"But I *really, really* love it."

"I know you love it, so I'm sure you'll do your practice. If not, we'll drop piano."

End of conversation. Do not listen to any more bargaining or negotiating. Simply reiterate what you said. Then leave him to follow through, or not follow through, and live with his decision.

Picky or Poor Eating Habits

You will find references elsewhere in this book to picky eating, but because it is such a common problem it merits its own section. Poor eating habits that start in early childhood can develop into serious eating disorders later in childhood and adolescence, so getting a handle on the problem early on is a wise thing to do. Even if serious disorders do not develop, frequent—sometimes lifelong—fighting over eating issues and the resultant bad feelings that can spoil mealtimes for the whole family are best prevented. Eating out can also be a frustrating and embarrassing experience when your child exhibits poor eating behaviors.

If he does not eat well at any meal, it could be because you are giving him portions that are too large for him, or because he is ingesting too many calories in between meals. Give him appropriate portions at meal times, make sure he is not getting too many calories at snack times, and do not insist he finish everything on his plate at every meal. In general he only needs three healthy meals each day, and two healthy, but small, snacks. When it comes to drinks, keep the sugar content to a minimum, and give him water to maintain hydration throughout the day.

Here are some typical poor eating habits any child might develop:

- **The Interrupter:** This child starts his meal but frequently interrupts it to do something that interests him. He takes an hour to finish.

- **The Grazer:** This child eats a little of his meal, leaves the table and does not finish. One hour later (or sooner) he needs a snack, which he may or may not finish. Another hour later (or sooner) he needs another snack or has another partial meal. Over the course of a day, he may start to eat eight to ten times or more, but rarely finishes what he starts.

- **The Selector:** This child will eat only a very small selection of foods, such as yogurt, potato chips, and chicken nuggets. He refuses to try anything else he is served. Or, he will eat more than three foods, but complains about (and refuses to eat) something he does not like at every meal.

In response to such habits, and hoping to meet their child's preferences and ensure he gets enough to eat, parents sometimes develop their own habits:

- **The Chef:** This parent prepares multiple meal choices hoping that the picky eater will at least eat something.

- **The Persuader:** This parent uses bribes or threats to get a picky eater to eat: "If you eat your beans you can have a popsicle." "If you don't eat your chicken, you can't have dessert."

- **The Preacher:** "There are millions of children in poor countries who are starving and would be glad to eat what you are refusing to eat. You should try eating rice for a day then you might be grateful."

If you or your child have developed any of the habits listed above, they are easy to change once you have decided it is time to do so. Use the End of Picky Eating technique.

A final note about behavior management: when it comes to discipline, you, like most parents, have probably heard that consistency is a *must*. However, do not worry if you think you cannot be consistent enough, or that you will start out being consistent, but then revert to inconsistency. I can assure you that when you have experienced the calm and peace that result from making positive behavioral change, you will never want to go back to your old ways. Once you see your consistency work, you will continue to be consistent.

Remember that by dealing in a clear, direct and firm way with all of the behaviors mentioned in this chapter, you are modeling how to behave as well as providing your child with necessary boundaries and limits. You are showing that you mean what you say and that while you understand his point, you are ultimately the one in charge. You are the leader he needs and although he may seem to want to be in control, he is neither equipped for—nor will he benefit from—taking on a leadership role. He will settle down once he realizes he will not be allowed to continue, or win, the fight with you.

CHAPTER 6

BEHAVIORS TO ENCOURAGE

Your child will respond well to having clear expectations set for the behaviors described in this chapter, although she may need extra encouragement or motivation when asked to start a new behavior that she is not excited about, or is afraid to try. However, setting an expectation is the easy part; the follow-through requires a certain amount of creativity and patience.

When you set an expectation, and your child does not comply, it can result in a sense of failure for both of you. However, this is not always a bad thing since valuable lessons can be learned from such failures. Let me explain what I mean:

Example: Suppose you tell your child you will no longer remind her to take her coat to school on cold days because she is old enough to remember for herself. The first time or two she "fails" to reach the expectation, you refrain from reminding her, and she endures the natural consequence of a couple of cold recesses. The next time she will surely remember to take her coat. Yes, the expectation initially results in "failure," but the resulting lesson taught by the natural consequence (not by you but by a cold recess) is priceless—and completely effective.

Children typically resist certain expectations. Do you have fond childhood memories of doing homework or chores, of going to bed before dark on a summer's night, or getting up on a cold winter's morning to go to school? I don't! Did you enjoy doing homework when you wanted to play outside with friends? I didn't! One tip for success is to first get your child's buy-in, especially when asking her to take on something she is reluctant to do. Rely on her natural sense of curiosity, playfulness, and desire to contribute as you set the expectation. Making it fun will help, as will appealing to her sense of fairness and willingness to learn.

Before setting an expectation, examine your own motives. You may be absolutely right in asking for behavioral change, but be sure you are asking for change for the right reasons. If you are expecting her to do something that is appropriate for her age, stage of development, and ability—that is great. But, if you are expecting her to make a change simply because you feel her poor behaviors reflect negatively on the way others perceive *you*, it is not. Requiring change purely for your benefit will bring disappointment for you both.

Chores

The word "chores" tends to send shivers up my spine and has about as much appeal as fingernails on a blackboard! If it has that effect on you, it may have the same negative impact on your child. Coming up with a new name, like "family help," might change that reaction and elicit stronger buy-in from her. If possible, begin encouraging chores when she is a toddler. Start with simple things that are within her ability to understand and perform, such as helping fold the socks, put silverware on the table, and pick up her toys at the end of the day. The goal is not to do the chore perfectly, but to show her how she can become a contributing member of the family. She will get better as she develops her physical coordination. However, if you did not start early, don't despair. Just begin now. Here are some tips that will help you prepare the whole family for the changes you plan to implement:

- Create a list of chores—with your children's input if you like, but you do not need their blessing—to be done every day and every week. Create a chore chart and post it somewhere in plain view. Some will be chores to be done by individuals, and some will be family chores for everyone to do.

- Explain to those involved what you are doing, and why. Encourage them to make suggestions about how each step could be carried out, and what each person's contributions could be.

- When all questions have been answered and whatever necessary materials have been acquired to carry out the chores, pick a start date (as soon as possible) and go for it. You may go through a honeymoon period for a week or two while the children enjoy the novelty, but you must be ready for when the initial novelty wears off.

If the children balk at doing certain chores, especially after the initial novelty turns into a drudge, there could be a good reason, so look for possible legitimate causes of resistance before you engage in behavior reinforcement. Perhaps the chores do not need to be done so often, or perhaps an older or younger child could, and should, be doing a particular chore. Ask for, and listen to, their input to see if some adjustments should be made.

- Have one child select everyone's chores from the family chores section of the chart for the coming week. With two or more children, rotate this privilege each week. If one child assigns the worst chores to a sibling, her turn (and payback!) will come next week. This method ensures that the children are fair in their selections and will learn the hard way if they take advantage of their position.

- Allow the children to trade with one another if schedules make certain chores hard to complete on time. Trading teaches them to negotiate and deal fairly with one another. Even if it looks like a fight is about to break out, step back and watch them develop these skills, since your interference might cause a fight where there might not otherwise be one. However, if you find that your ten-year-old always selects the hardest chores for the four-year-old—who cannot possibly do them—you will have to step in. Let your older child know what a four-year-old is able to do and instruct her to pick from that list only. She might be giving out the hard tasks just to be awkward, but assume that she is doing it out of ignorance.

- If your children criticize or judge each other's performance, treat it as you would sibling rivalry.

- If you need to periodically encourage or motivate your children to complete their chores, be creative in letting a natural consequence influence the outcome. In the absence of a natural consequence, create one that will have the desired effect.

- Find ways to positively acknowledge and reward the efforts they make.

Example: You have started a new job and have to leave home earlier in the morning and think your seven-year-old is ready to start taking on more chores. You and she have agreed that she will make her own lunch for school and help her three-year-old brother with his breakfast every day. You make sure everything she needs is within her reach and that she can accomplish both tasks. Things go well for a week. Then she forgets about her brother and focuses only on getting her lunch ready; she says there is not enough time to do both. You tell her you will get her up ten minutes earlier to give her more time and if this does not give her enough time, you will get her up 20 minutes earlier, and so on, with the compensating earlier bedtime until she feels she can handle both tasks. Although you do not mention it, you know that she will miss part of her favorite TV show by going to bed earlier. When she realizes this, it may be enough motivation to get her to help her brother, but if not, make sure you follow through. When she complains, remind her that you are sending her to bed early so she has adequate time to get ready in the morning. If she is able to help her brother, the later bedtime can be reinstated and she can watch her show. Linking her behavior with something she enjoys should end any resistance.

Tidying Up Toys

It sometimes seems that a child's small size is completely unrelated to the giant-sized mess she can generate. I always considered my short legs a bonus when I had young children because picking things off the floor was an easier reach for me than for my long-legged friends! Joking aside, toys and general mess can become an eyesore, if not a hazard and it is best to get a handle on this problem early on. But regardless of your child's age, it is possible to teach her how to be tidy. The first trick is to start small and set an expectation that she clear only part of the mess. Areas like the dining room or family room can be good places to begin since they are often the hardest hit. Alternatively, focusing on particular items such as books, clothes, sports equipment, or toys will make tidying up more manageable. Leave her room until last because you can close the door and not be bothered by the mess.

Example: Once you have picked either the area or item to be targeted, let your child know your plans. Explain that from now on you expect everyone to pick up after themselves so the house will be neater and more comfortable. Work out with her the areas or items she is responsible for and when (during the day or during the week) she will tidy up. Incorporate as much of her input as you can to increase her buy-in. Once she clearly understands what is expected, agree on a start date and observe her follow-through.

Outcome #1: She picks up after herself as agreed and expected, and gets ample recognition for her efforts.

Outcome #2: She does not tidy up at all, or makes a half-hearted effort. Make the observation (do not complain) that she did not do what was agreed to, and tell her that she will have another chance to do it tomorrow at the same time. If she follows through, be sure to acknowledge and praise her.

Outcome #3: She does not follow through the following day after being reminded. The best technique to use for this outcome is The Bag.

Once she follows through with tidying up her toys, praise her for her great work. This activity should soon become habitual.

Toilet Training

While it is appropriate to cover toilet training in a chapter that covers the development of positive behaviors, your child is not behaving negatively if she is not toilet trained by some predetermined age. In addition to reading what I have to say, I encourage you to do your own research by speaking to your pediatrician for medical guidance on this important developmental milestone.

Because each child reaches the toilet training stage on her own schedule, I do not want to set your expectations at a particular age. However, two signs will help you decide she is ready. One is when she lets you know she has a wet or dirty diaper. This indicates that she has the necessary awareness of her bladder and bowels to begin the training process. Another sign is curiosity in bathroom activity, yours and that of other family members. Allow her to watch you "perform," and see the results of your performance, or wave bye-bye as she flushes such results away. One word of warning: children who like to give human waste a royal sendoff tend to also give other things the royal flush: watches, rings, toilet paper, and other sundry or cherished items. Do not be embarrassed about the frequent visits from your friendly plumber—numerous other parents have survived such embarrassment.

Once you see these signs of readiness, prepare for the training process, which might take a few months. You might need to change your routines and temporarily free up some time to accommodate the extra attention your child needs. Make this joint effort as much fun as you possibly can. Being overly serious or wedded to a goal that is yours rather than hers will slow progress, or stop it altogether when she picks up on your tension and resists you.

Start by getting her own potty chair and let her lug it around at home. The more familiar she can become with it, the more quickly she will feel comfortable about the whole process. She may "use" it with a diaper on; that is fine, she is just rehearsing. See if she is willing to use it without a diaper. Let her go at her own pace and admire anything she might randomly produce while enthroned; I call such random results *unintentional* potty productions.

When she seems comfortable sitting on the potty chair without a diaper, she may be ready for the next step: sitting on the potty for *intentional* potty productions. Here is how you can help her. Either sit her on the potty at regular intervals or wait until she indicates by words or body language that she is ready to perform, and then sit her down. Stay with her and chat or read if she wants you to. Otherwise leave her alone and wait until she is done. Then help her clean up.

Always take her lead. If she seems to regress and has more accidents or does not want to use the potty, wait until she seems ready to try again. There is not much you can do to rush her. As much as you may want her out of diapers, remember she will no longer be a "baby" once she is trained. You may even go through a time of grieving what you both have left behind. Relax, and allow her to progress naturally. Once she is proficient with the potty chair, suggest she use the toilet and help her if she is eager to do so. Again, she will move ahead when she is good and ready, so follow her lead.

While she is going through the toilet training process, be playful with her about such things as transferring from diapers to pull-ups or from pull-ups to underwear. Of course, make a big fuss when letting her choose the kind of underwear she likes, and let her wear it whether or not she is toilet trained. Let her wear her underwear over or under diapers or clothes if she wants to. It doesn't matter as long as she is experimenting and showing interest in, and comfort with, the process.

Sleeping Alone

If your child has habitually been sharing your bed for all or part of the night, there may come a time when sleeping alone or with your partner without interruption becomes a priority. Perhaps you are planning another pregnancy and want to get your child into her bed before the baby arrives. Maybe you think it is time for her to sleep alone. Whatever your reason, the nature and length of this transition will depend on what she has become accustomed to, and how you approach the change. Here are three typical scenarios:

- Your child has been sleeping in her own crib and is transitioning to a junior or regular bed.
- She has been sleeping in bed with you and now you want her to sleep in her own crib or bed all night.
- She has been sleeping in her own bed, but will not go to sleep without you beside her and wakes up every time you try to sneak away.

All of these situations can be approached the same way. Wait for a time when you have three or four nights in a row during which you can make the transition. You may get less sleep than usual, so keep your days relatively free of commitments. Prepare with your partner and agree on what role you will each play and how you can support one another. When you are ready, set an expectation with her if she is old enough to understand. If you think she is too young, it is still a good idea to explain, since she probably understands more than you think. Tell her you are going to put her in her own bed that night, and she will sleep there all night. Let her know if she gets up and comes into your bed, you will take her back. Keep the message short and simple, and your tone kind and firm. When evening comes, go through the usual bedtime routine and then proceed as you have said. One of several things will happen:

Outcome #1: She goes to sleep without a peep and sleeps all night. This might surprise you beyond belief, but it could happen.

Outcome #2: She immediately gets up and comes to find you. Gently take her back to bed, again reminding her that she is old enough to sleep in her bed all night. Keep doing this, even if it takes an hour or more, until she falls asleep. Eventually she will stay in bed. If she gets up during the night and tries to get into bed with you, put her back as you did before.

Outcome #3: She stays in her bed, but screams in protest. Go in every ten or fifteen minutes and let her know you are there, and say the same soothing thing each time. Eventually sleep will settle the issue.

You may be surprised how easy it actually is when you decide it is time for her to sleep through the night in her own bed. Sometimes these changes are harder on you than they are on her because she was ready but you were not. Once you make the decision to change, it shows her that you are ready, and things may just fall into place.

Some parents barricade their child in with a baby gate or by shutting the bedroom door when making the transition. I do not suggest this as your first approach because barring your child from contact with you may unnecessarily alarm her. I understand that it means less work for you if she is contained, but it might actually take longer for the transition to take effect. If she has full access to you, with your firm and gentle holding to the expectation serving as her barricade, she will feel safe and transition more quickly. Whatever method you choose depends on your particular situation and what you are willing to do.

Value-driven Behaviors

Most of us want our children to grow up with value-driven behaviors such as sharing, kindness, generosity, honesty, politeness, respect and manners. We want to give them every opportunity to succeed in a world that requires them to be humane, social, and thoughtful. For the most part, these are not behaviors you can simply teach, like cooking or catching a ball; you must model them so your child can unconsciously absorb them. It is also important to understand the distinction between her developmental readiness to engage in value-driven behaviors, and your need as a parent to respond to social expectations that she do so. She is developmentally ready to engage in these behaviors when she does them without much prompting, or readily does them when prompted. Value-driven behaviors require a fairly sophisticated level of social awareness, and she needs to have developed the ability to empathize with others in order to engage in them autonomously. This readiness occurs somewhere between the ages of four and seven. Younger children can mimic the behaviors, but will not be able to initiate them until they are developmentally ready.

Once you see readiness signs, briefly explain the benefits that engaging in the behavior can bring to her and others. Then let her give it a try. If she is ready she will feel proud about accomplishing something new. If you do not see signs of readiness but feel compelled to make her demonstrate kindness and generosity, be honest about whether this is for you or her.

Perhaps "selfish" or "unkind" behavior causes you embarrassment, or you want to impress someone with her "correct" behavior. However, if you insist she try, be sure to use gentle encouragement, and if she strongly resists, do not push. If she continues to resist your efforts, withdraw from the fight and try again when she is older. In the meantime, make sure she has the chance to watch you model these gentle behaviors.

Sharing

If your child is old enough, but shows poor sharing behavior, ask yourself why that might be. Has she been raised to expect to receive but not give? Do the adults around her model sharing behaviors or not? If she has had little exposure to the sharing behaviors of others, she will have little to copy. But by the time she is six or seven, she is old enough to learn, and you can assume she is ready. Here are a few insights and tips that might help:

Practice sharing with her by having her select one of her possessions and suggest she share it with you. She will find sharing with you easier than sharing with a peer or sibling. Once she has shared with you (with much praise), tell her you are sure she is ready to share with someone else. Give her a choice about *what* she will share, not *whether* she will share. When she has tried sharing this way a few times and has discovered the sky has not fallen, her resistance will diminish as her confidence and pride grow.

Another strategy is to tell her that because you trust her, you are going to let her share something special of yours. It does not matter what it is, or whether or not she can make use of it, because all you are doing is giving her the opportunity to experience how the receiver of sharing feels. If she feels honored to hold something of yours for a while and return it, it will help her learn that someone else can do the same with her possessions.

Sharing requires a certain level of trust, so your child will share with people she knows and trusts before sharing with strangers. Sharing can also evoke feelings of competition. Therefore she might share quite happily with adults or with other children, before she shares with siblings. Help her with easy sharing before expecting her to progress to difficult sharing.

Kindness and Generosity

Let me define exactly what I mean by kindness and generosity. Kindness is when a person makes an effort to empathize with another person's situation and behaves in such a way as to bring some benefit to the other, while to do so may or may not bring personal benefit. Although generosity is similar and can be defined as giving one's time and attention to another person, it also suggests a generosity of spirit.

Again, modeling the behavior is the most effective way to instill kindness and generosity in your child. But other great ways are to give her the opportunity to help you and other family members, as well as letting her participate in community service when she is old enough. Be sure she understands, however, that giving without limits is not healthy. Many people have learned only to *give*, but not to *ask* for what they need and they have a hard time accepting help when it is offered. Resentment and low self-esteem can be the result of being generous to a fault. Teach her to set appropriate boundaries with generosity and show her how to meet her own needs before extending generosity to others. The best way you can teach her is by modeling how you limit your kindness and generosity to manageable levels—tell her how and when you do this so she sees actual examples of what you mean.

Honesty

Like most parents, you probably want your child to be honest, and it is natural to feel concern if you catch her in a lie or otherwise behaving dishonestly. If that happens, what is the best way to handle it? First, determine whether or not the lie is intentional. Up to the age of four or five (and sometimes even six), a child may not even understand what a lie is. This is particularly likely if her family lives by its value to be honest. She will have had little experience of being lied to or seeing others behaving dishonestly. Her lying may be evidence of an overactive imagination, childish fabrication, or a way to make herself seem more important and powerful than she feels. By the time she is six years old, however, she is mature enough to understand lying as a concept and can make a conscious decision to lie if she chooses to.

If a child who is raised in an environment where everyone behaves honestly suddenly begins to lie, first consider that her lying may be symptomatic of underlying stress. Has she recently changed schools or made another sort of move? Is the family undergoing a transition, or is someone ill? Ask her teacher if she has noticed her lying at school or if something alarming or unusual has happened to one of her classmates, which she might be trying to make sense of. If you cannot find a root cause, calmly point out to her that she is lying and ask why. She may be repeating interesting stories she heard from another child, fantasizing, wishing, or elaborating. Be sure she understands what it means to lie, and why you do not want her to do that. Reassure her that telling the truth will not get her into trouble with you—and then remember not to get upset with her if she tells the truth and it is something that upsets you. When she lets you know of something dishonest she has done, thank her for being forthright. However, if appropriate, you can still follow through with a consequence for the dishonest behavior (see example on the following page.)

If she has been raised in an environment in which people sometimes say one thing and do another, she will be able to intentionally tell a lie at a much earlier age. She will have understood, at a visceral level, that such behavior either gets her something she wants (such as praise or attention), or allows her to avoid something she does not want (such as doing chores or being sent to the principal's office).

Fear of retribution and fear of disappointing a parent or other respected person can also cause a child to lie. If she has been punished harshly for misbehaving in the past, she will do everything possible to hide similar misbehavior in the future, including lying. If you catch her lying, do not punish her harshly, because it will only reinforce future dishonest behavior as she tries to avoid the punishment. Instead, follow through with a consequence that will help her learn that lying does not pay.

Example: You have an agreement that every Saturday morning she is to clean her room before she can play. One Saturday she tells you she has cleaned her room, and rushes out to join in a game with her friends. You subsequently find her room has not been touched. When you confront her with your discovery, she admits she was eager to play and lied to you. Rather than taking away a privilege, grounding her, or preaching about honesty, require that she not only clean her room, but also a common area in the home to make up for lying.

I also strongly encourage you not to be angry with, or punish her if she lies about a grade. It is more important to focus on what she did not understand about the material and get her the help so she can keep up with her work. However, remind her that lying is not acceptable behavior and give her a related consequence, such as learning 25 new spelling words. The consequence may be unpleasant for her, but it is a positive learning experience for two reasons: one is that lying does not pay and the other is that she improves her spelling. Assure her she can come to you or her teacher if she has trouble with schoolwork again.

If her lying becomes habitual, you can find no reason for it, and using behavioral techniques has not worked, seeking professional help is the best course of action.

Politeness and Respect

Parents often ask me what they can do about impoliteness, disrespect, and "attitude" problems with their children. Here is some food for thought:

Do you generally behave in a polite and respectful way yourself, modeling these behaviors for your child, or do you tend to *tell* her to be polite and show respect, when you do not behave that way? She will not know how to be polite and respectful merely by being told. If, on the other hand, she is impolite or disrespectful despite plenty of good modeling by you, her behaviors may be symptomatic of something else. Perhaps she feels like a failure, or inferior. She may be rude or disrespectful and putting others down in order to make herself feel less insecure or helpless. Assume that she feels bad about herself in some way and engage her in conversations about her life and friends while using the Active Listening technique. Doing this will strengthen her sense of self-worth. As her attitude towards herself improves, so will her attitude towards others. You can also make a safe assumption that although you model honesty and respect, she may simply need extra guidance. Talk to her about your concern over her apparent rudeness and give her examples of when and how to behave respectfully and politely. Perhaps she needs you to tutor her. If you think about it, people who habitually behave respectfully and politely make it look easy. But it definitely takes practice.

If your child is approaching late childhood or early adolescence, and she is developing what you see as an attitude problem, there may be several reasons. First of all, it is unlikely that she is behaving that way in order to be punished or to deliberately disappoint you. She may instead be feeling the unconscious but powerful developmental urge to separate from her family of origin and gravitate towards her friends—her new "family." As she does this, it may be easier for her to push her old family away, ignore them, depersonalize them, or convince herself they are not worth being nice to.

Separating from the family of origin could be too anxiety-provoking if she allows herself to feel the sadness, disloyalty or unkindness she would naturally experience as she leaves them behind. To some degree it is necessary for her to distance herself emotionally (at least temporarily) in order to leave childhood behind. In the process it is easier to fight you than to grieve losing you. Having said that however, she still lives at home and rules about respect and politeness still exist. Remind her that you are not relaxing your standards about behavior, but that you do understand the confusion that can occur while going through the pre-adolescent and adolescent stages.

Remember to demonstrate politeness and respect by your own behaviors, and teach her how to be polite and respectful if she seems to be lacking the skills.

Manners

Manners can be modeled as well as taught as a skill. For example, you can teach your child how to hold a knife and fork and how to eat with her mouth closed. You can teach her not to push in line, to hold a door for someone after going through, and to say "please" and "thank you appropriately. These lessons are taught in the same way as any other lessons: by demonstrating how to do it, providing her opportunities to practice, and by rewarding progress.

Decide which manners you would like her to learn, and then simply show her what you do so she can follow your example. Positive Reinforcement is all she will need to remember the manners you teach her.

CHAPTER 7

REINFORCEMENT TECHNIQUES

This chapter covers a variety of behavioral reinforcement techniques designed to help you retain your sanity (important!) as you gain control over your child's behaviors. Some techniques can be used to eliminate aggressive, dangerous, annoying, or embarrassing behaviors while others encourage the development of wanted behaviors. Refer to the Techniques Index on page 14 to find the page number for the suggested technique.

When using any reinforcement technique, take note of the tone of your voice. Even if you learn and implement the technique well, your tone will reveal any negative emotion you may be feeling and reduce your effectiveness. If you find yourself using the chosen technique repeatedly with little or no effect, you should probably try a different one, or consider that you may have picked the wrong one, or be using the right one incorrectly.

Remember that children are a long way from being adults and have much growing and developing yet to do. Your child is not just a short-limbed adult! It helps if you develop and maintain a compassionate perspective and remain calm as you deal with his negative behaviors. When you became a parent, you accepted the responsibility of raising him, and being compassionate and patient with him is crucial. If he fell and cut his knee, you would not get upset. You would put on a bandage and make sure he was okay. It is the same with misbehaving. He may be unaware of what he is doing and needs your patient help.

Techniques that Encourage Behavior

Positive Reinforcement

Catching your child in the act of behaving well, and positively noticing or acknowledging it, is not as easy as it sounds, but making a conscious effort to do so will produce great results. This is important because the brain registers the positive. For example, instead of saying, "Don't hit your brother," say "Hitting your brother hurts him." Instead of saying, "Don't put your clothes on the floor," say "Put your clothes in the hamper." Instead of saying, "Don't leave your toys lying around," say "Picking up your toys would be really helpful."

One of the reasons it is difficult to catch him in the act of behaving well is that when he behaves as expected, he does not draw attention to himself in the same way he does when misbehaving. You can easily overlook good behaviors, but inadvertently reinforce poor behaviors by giving then negative attention. Whether positive or negative, attention is attention and that is what every child needs and wants. There are many ways to positively encourage good behaviors. Some of the following basic characteristics of Positive Reinforcement will strengthen any of the techniques you choose:

- The younger your child (up to age five), the sooner the reward should come after the behavior. He does not have a great attention span or tons of patience! Saying he will get more toys on his birthday if he does what you ask will not motivate him as much as telling him you will read an extra book after he has brushed his teeth, put on his pajamas, and is ready for bed. Besides, you probably will not remember to follow through with the promise about his birthday. Your task is to help a young child make an immediate connection between his behavior and your positive acknowledgement.

- An older child (six to ten) can get his reward in increments since he is better able to delay gratification. For example, each day he accomplishes the goal behavior, he earns a good behavior coupon. After getting a certain number of coupons he can cash them in for a reward.
- Give unexpected praise and acknowledgement. For example, say something like "I've noticed you've been extra patient and helpful with your sister all day, and I'm really pleased with you." Even though you have not asked for that behavior, it lets him know you have noticed.
- If you have rewarded your child for certain good or expected behaviors do not take the reward away, even if he misbehaves. Treat the poor behavior with another technique instead of rescinding the reward.
- Do something special: spend time alone with him; arrange a sleepover with his best friend; plan an overnight or weekend camping trip with the family; take a trip to the water-park or the zoo; go bowling; or out to his favorite restaurant.
- Create a "reward box" with all kinds of activities he enjoys and have him select one as a reward when he has earned it.

Caveats to Positive Reinforcement

I have a few caveats about Positive Reinforcement that I would like to point out:

First, young children definitely need to be given external reward and reinforcement in order to develop self esteem as well as to understand which behaviors are acceptable and which are not. But as they grow older, they should be encouraged to shift the balance to utilizing their own internally-driven capability for motivation and reward rather than continuing to rely on external factors.

Second, children should be encouraged and expected to contribute to the family and—later on in childhood and adolescence—to their community without expecting any reward for doing so. This kind of contribution needs no reward other than the sense of pride or generosity that they get from giving to others who are less fortunate, or from simply giving because they are able to or want to.

Allowance and Earning Money

The third caveat to Positive Reinforcement is actually a technique in and of itself. The issue of allowances is a topic which frequently comes up when I speak to parents. They ask whether children should be given an allowance as motivation to do chores or improve their behaviors. They also ask should money earned this way be taken away for not complying with what is expected. My answers to these questions are: there is no need to use money as incentive or reward for things your child is expected to do, or for behaving well. But if you have given him money for these reasons, it should not be taken away. Instead, I suggest you stop the practice and when the money earned from it is gone, give your child other ways to earn. Perhaps he could earn money by doing things he would not normally be expected to do. For example, if he is not normally expected to wash the car, sweep the garage, or do one-off tasks like that, then certainly pay him an agreed-upon amount if you choose. However, should he misbehave, money earned from doing such tasks was earned honestly and cannot be taken away.

Explain ahead of time what money means, how he can earn it and how he can save it. Having an allowance can certainly be used to teach such lessons. Give him a weekly allowance, and have him agree to save a small percentage of it while he chooses to do what he wants with the remainder. That way he can spend as well as learn how to save and enjoy the benefits from doing both.

Sticker Charts

The younger your child, the more eager he will be to use a sticker chart and see tangible and colorful proof of his good behavior. Older children can enjoy them too. Here are a few fundamentals for you to consider when using the sticker chart approach.

- Be clear about what your child will get a sticker for, and always put up a sticker when he has done what was expected. For example, "Every time you're ready to leave for school on time, you'll be able to choose a sticker when you get home. When you have five stickers, you can have a reward."

- There should be no conditions attached to getting the sticker or the reward other than doing the expected behavior. Even if he misbehaves over something else, yet does the required behavior, he gets the sticker. If you take stickers away from what he has earned, you will confuse him and reduce the effectiveness of the sticker system.

- When he has reached the agreed-upon number of stickers, deliver the reward. I would suggest you keep the reward simple and non-materialistic, but something he really enjoys.

Modeling

Modeling simply means that you teach by the way you behave. Children are primed to copy the behaviors of the people around them, especially those in caretaking roles. So if you behave in ways you would like your child to behave—such as being kind, honest, and respectful—you will need to spend little time teaching him how to behave in those ways. However, if you behave poorly, yet expect him to behave well, you create an expectation that will end in disappointment. Don't expect more from him than you would from yourself.

Of course, no one is perfect and you will no doubt model behaviors you do not want him to copy from time to time. You can easily confuse him by what you say if it is contrary to how you behave. Perhaps you break the speed limit, use recreational drugs, swear, or lose your temper—all the while admonishing him not to do such things. Hopefully, when he points this out, you can listen respectfully and answer with humility. But since it is not possible to live a perfect life, be realistic and tolerant as you set standards for his behaviors. Talk to him about how you sometimes struggled with your own behaviors at his age (and still do). Not only is it good for him to know you are human and make mistakes, but it will also help him feel a little less disappointed in himself when he messes up.

Active Listening

Active Listening is different from normal listening—which is what we do most of the time. With normal listening we hear what is said, we understand the overall meaning, and the speaker may or may not come away from the exchange feeling understood. Active listening is a skill that must be learned and sharpened. When actively listening, we hear what is said and understand the overall meaning, but in addition to that we show the speaker that we have heard and understood any deeper meaning and message he may be trying to convey. Here are the three components to Active Listening that make it the powerful technique that it is:

Asking for clarification: "Did you say your coach will have the information for you in May or in June?

Mirroring: Repeat back to him what you understood. "So you were told that if you want to join the soccer team, you must have enough time to attend three practices each week and play in a game each weekend, right?"

Validating: Validate what you hear. "I'm sorry you lost your homework and had to stay in at recess. After waking up with a cold too! Sounds like today hasn't been your best day."

All of these comments and questions give your child the clear message that you hear what he is telling you, you understand him, *and* you are totally engaged in the conversation. The message he receives is that he is valuable to you, loved by you, and his life is worth your undivided attention. Those are powerful messages that go a long way towards building his self-worth, as well as building a strong relationship with you.

Example: Your child badly wants something (such a common occurrence!) and is agitatedly telling you that he really, really, *really* has to have that particular toy. Travis has that toy. Tyler has that toy. Everyone has that toy. He just *has* to have it and is getting more and more vociferous as he explains why. Do not interrupt him, but wait for him to pause for a breath. Then in a calm, non-judgmental voice, tell him that you know he *really, really* wants that toy and that it must be *so* frustrating for him not to have it like Travis and Tyler, but you are not going to buy it. Mirror his angst and empathize with him to convey your sincerity. Sometimes that is all he needs. Since he has been heard and understood, do not be surprised if it absolutely stops him in his tracks

If he keeps it up, you patiently keep it up, too, and continue to calmly agree that it must be frustrating, but no, you are not buying that toy. It is important *not* to soften the message in other ways, such as buying a different toy, promising to buy that particular toy at some other time, letting him earn the money to buy it, or suggesting another solution. Doing that might make *you* feel better, but it does not help him understand that he cannot always get what he wants from you every time he asks. Such an approach might result in negotiating, which is not a good habit to encourage. When he has repeated himself a couple more times, tell him the subject is closed and just drop it. Ignore his pleas, move on with what you were doing, and direct his focus to another activity. After the incident is completely over, you can talk to him about how he can get things he wants in the future.

Use of Humor and Creativity

If you have ever trained animals, even a family pet, you will know how well they respond to your efforts if you do two things: (1) make use of what is already part of their natural behavior, and; (2) make it enjoyable for them. The same approach works with your child since his natural enthusiasm tends to allow him to enjoy so may things. Making a game out of a routine or using creative ways to motivate him, can be such fun that he might not even know he is complying with your request. To the extent that you are comfortable doing so, let him lead the way with creativity and humor. Some of us parents are a long way from remembering what it is like to be a creative and imaginative five-year-old!

Example #1: He resists putting on his pajamas. Suggest he find a funny way to wear them: inside out, upside down, back to front. Start the ball rolling and let him run with it. Suggest he come up with ideas for how the whole family should wear their pajamas. Have a "switch pajama" night. Go along with his ideas. After all, who outside the family is going to see what you or anyone else looks like?

Example #2: If he resists setting the table for dinner when you ask, make it into a game and ask for his ideas (such as giving each family member only one utensil, seeing who can eat with only one hand, etc.) Not only does this approach strengthen his creative muscles, it can also be a great mood-lightener.

I like to include teaching in the humor and creative category—and I'm talking about your child teaching *you*, as well as the other way around. When you encourage him to teach you, several things happen. First, he forgets he is doing a chore or complying with a request he might resist. Second, he gets a rare chance to show off his abilities and be in charge. Third, you get a front row seat at his performance. And fourth, it improves your relationship with him. How can you lose? Try this approach with something new, or with something he normally dislikes doing.

Example #3: He dislikes making his bed, so ask him to show you how to make your bed while you watch. Don't worry if it is not done well, or even partly well. The object of this exercise is for him to be in control and benefit from being the teacher. While he learns or improves his skill, make the most of his performance. Show lots of curiosity. Ask him to let you do it with his help if you make mistakes. Put him in charge of bed making for anyone in the family who is willing to let him show them. Soon enough he will wear the bed-making role proudly and the fight will be over.

Getting Buy-in

Every manager knows that if he wants to make changes, he will be more successful if he first clearly defines the goal, takes the time to get buy-in from his direct reports, and lets them reach the goal in the best way they know how. He may still be able to force some changes through without taking this approach, but it will be a slow, uphill climb.

When guiding your child through behavioral changes, your role is much the same as that of a manager. Required changes come about more quickly once the goal is clear, your child has an opportunity to give his input, and you leave him to accomplish the task. As an added benefit, he will feel good about himself. You are not asking for his permission to make a change, nor are you expecting total approval and, of course, sometimes you still must implement changes that are unpopular. But including him in the process will often garner buy-in when resistance would otherwise be the response.

Do you remember being six years old and having no power or authority? Can you remember what it was like to be told what to do fifty times each day? Think how great it would have been if someone had actually *asked* instead of *told* you to do something? How powerful you would have felt! You can tap into your child's enormous desire and ability to master something new, to be creative and helpful, if you first *ask* him how he can help. It might be easy for him to resist *your* ideas, but it is more difficult for him to resist *his* ideas!

Example: Your eight-year-old is tired after school, and although he loves his Tuesday and Thursday gymnastic classes and gets so much out of them, he is never ready when you want to leave. This has been going on for months. You are fed up with the situation and do not know what to do. Try the following by customizing the words you use, but keep the intent the same:

"Jamie, I've got a problem and I could really use your help. Perhaps you could come up with some ideas that might work." (You are appealing to his innate sense of curiosity and probably have his attention. If this is a new way for you to approach him, he will probably be fully engaged.) "The problem is this: I've been trying to get us out of the house in time for gymnastics every week, and I seem to be getting nowhere. We're always late, I end up nagging at you to get ready, and we're usually mad at each other when we finally get in the car." (He is probably nodding in agreement by now.) "If you really want to continue with gymnastics, perhaps you could come up with some ideas for us to get there on time. If we can't find a solution, I'll have to assume you don't want to continue, and you can drop the class. What do you think?" (Now you are creating a consequence and appealing to his natural tendency to want to help, as well as to his sense of fairness.) Assume he wants to cooperate and give him time to come up with some ideas. Listen when he presents them to you, try them out, and see how it goes.

Outcome #1: His ideas and planning were excellent, the follow-through worked well, and the problem is solved.

Outcome #2: Although his ideas and planning were excellent, the follow-through is not, and when Tuesday rolls around, nothing changes. Do not take him to gymnastics. Give him a reminder that you will try again on Thursday, but that if things do not change, you will understand he does not want to continue the classes. When Thursday arrives, he is ready to go. The solution is working.

Outcome #3: Tuesday has come and gone, along with the missed class and your reminder, but he is still not ready on Thursday. Let him know that his behavior is telling you he no longer wants to take gymnastics classes and will not be going any more. He may complain, but do not give in. He has had plenty of opportunity to show that he wants to continue and has demonstrated his decision through his behavior.

Although it is not always possible—or even necessary—to get his buy-in, always consider the option since it can be helpful. By getting buy-in, you are handing him some ownership in the change, and he is more likely to cooperate.

Choice

In order to have a positive influence on changing your child's behaviors, consider giving him a choice. By doing that, you are showing respect and allowing some freedom. You are also raising the level of his buy-in and, thus, his ultimate compliance. Choice is a good thing in many ways, but giving him the wrong choice, too many choices too often, or a choice under the wrong conditions can be counterproductive. Only allow choices you can live with. There is no point in giving him a choice between two things when you are only prepared to accept one. That is a trap, not a choice! Also, be sure to use choices appropriately, because if wrongly used you run the risk of your child developing the habit of negotiating. The suggestions below will help you make proper use of choices.

No matter what his age, if he has a meltdown over making a choice and seems to be in an agony of indecision, there may be a couple of reasons. Perhaps you have previously challenged or opposed his choices (so now he doubts his ability to make an acceptable selection), or you have given him too complex a selection for his age. Remember to keep it simple and give him choices you can live with. Here are some guidelines you can follow when giving your child the opportunity to choose:

- He is ready for simple choices from twelve to fifteen months old. He can choose whether or not he wants what you are offering. For example, you ask if he would like some juice and his options are "yes" or "no." That is about all a child of that age can manage. Giving more choice than that before he is ready results in him wanting every option, and feeling deprived when only allowed one choice.

- After that, he can progress to what is sometimes referred to as the illusion of choice. Although he is beyond the yes/no stage, he is not old enough to judge the ramifications of his choice, so you must make it simple for him and make whichever way he chooses right. For example, "Would you like to take your bath before supper or after supper?" He gets the opportunity to choose *when* he takes a bath, but not *if*. Either way, he gets the bath.

- Minimize the number of options you give him so he is not overwhelmed. Asking a four-year-old if he would like to have his bath before or after he picks up toys, or a bedtime book instead of a bath, or a movie before or after the bath will probably send him into a tailspin—and you too, since that's quite a lot to remember! It is better just to give him an either/or choice, such as, "After you pick up your toys and have your bath, would you like a book or a short video before bed?" After the age of six or so, children can usually handle a multiple-choice selection.

- Only give him choices that are appropriate for his age. You might allow your twelve-year-old to choose whether your family goes on vacation next year to Grandma's (a plane ride away), or to visit his cousins in the next state (a car drive away). However, you would not give the same choice to a three-year-old, who *could* make the choice, but would not be able to weigh the pros and cons. By the same token, do not give your twelve-year-old choices that you would give to a five-year-old or you will get rolling eyes and withering looks, and rightly so! He will feel patronized.

At times your child might fight making a choice because he finds it easier for you to do it for him. The problem with choosing for him is that he might fight your selection, and then he is fighting *you* instead of solving the internal dilemma he might have experienced had *he* been left to make the choice. Making choices helps him develop the ability to weigh the pros and cons of his selection—so necessary for developing the ability to make decisions. Letting him make his own choices also increases ownership in his behavior, as well as increasing the accountability for the consequences of his actions. When he makes a choice and it turns out to be the wrong one, praise his effort. It was a choice made out of an honest lack of experience, and he will have learned a lesson about making poor choices. The lesson, not the outcome, was a success.

Reframing

Reframing is an effective and simple technique to use, but might require that you change your words and phrases in order to accentuate the positive.

Avoid threats or bribes and keep your tone friendly and neutral. Reframing can be a helpful technique when setting expectations and using consequences. Here are some common mistakes:

- The words "you need" as in "You need to take your bath" are red flags to most children because they quickly figure out that it is about *your* need, not *theirs.*
- Shouting, or heavily emphasizing, the word "now" as in "Take your bath NOW!" can also spark your child's defiance because it puts him on the defensive.
- If you tend to say, "If you don't take your bath, then you can't watch your show," know that it sounds like a threat, because it *is.* The words "if/then" are usually parentheses around a threat or a bribe, so avoid them if you can.
- If you tend to say, "If you take your bath, then I'll let you watch your show," know that it sounds like a bribe, because it *is.* He is being held accountable for his actions by you, rather than by himself or by a consequence that he cannot argue with.

It is best to avoid delivering either a threat or a bribe. Instead, set an expectation: "You can watch your show when you've had your bath." The expectation lies in the words "you can" and "when. The follow-through lies in the fact that he gets his show *only* when he's had the bath. No bath, no show. His choice.

Example: Brushing his teeth is the last part of the bedtime routine for your child before he gets into bed to read. However you must constantly remind him. You have decided that he is old enough to remember to brush his teeth. Tell him in a voice that is firm and matter-of-fact: "I think you're old enough now to remember to brush your teeth, and you certainly don't need me to remind you any longer. From now on you can do them just before you go to bed to read." See if he has any meaningful ideas, incorporate them wherever possible to get buy-in, and start the very next night.

Outcome #1: He does his teeth and gets into bed to read.

Outcome #2: He gets into bed, but has not done his teeth. Remind to brush his teeth so he can read. He brushes his teeth and gets into bed to read.

Outcome #3: If he still has not done his teeth and it is time for bed, tell him it is now too late to read. Put him to bed and say goodnight in your usual way. He may not have earned his reading time, but he always gets your affection. Then leave him and ignore any pleas. If he gets up to get a book, or to complain, repeat your message that he can read tomorrow night when he has done his teeth. Then send him back to bed. This may go on for a while, but keep it up and you will eventually succeed.

In case you are concerned that he will never do his teeth, try this approach: tell him that while his teeth are un-brushed, they are also unprotected, so he cannot have sugary food or drink. Once he brushes his teeth—and thus protects them—the restrictions are lifted. This message hits home when the next snack or meal consists of food and drink without sugar!

Reframing is often used in combination with Setting Expectations and when preparing to use the Natural Consequences or Created Consequences techniques.

Redirecting

Redirecting simply refers to providing an alternative activity on which to focus your child's attention from something you don't want him to do to something that is acceptable. This is an effective beginner's technique— beginner parent and beginner child—although it can be useful at any age. For your 12- to 18-month-old, it should be all you need to head off unwanted behavior or to stop it once it starts. However, should you need a stronger technique, I suggest trying Time Out with a Toddler.

Example: Your two-year-old has happily discovered that banging a fork on the dining table produces dents, and he wants to make dents everywhere. He has no idea that he is causing damage; he has just made an exciting discovery! Punishing him is not appropriate. So give him some old pieces of wood to bang on where it will not cause any damage. Encourage him to make as many dents as he can in each piece of wood and tell him that the wood is his own special place to make dents; nobody else can make dents there, unless he gives permission. Be prepared to display his dented artwork in prominent places for weeks to come!

There is usually a way you can convert unwanted behaviors to appropriate ones. How you handle it is what makes the difference. Keep trying, use your ingenuity, and enjoy the results.

In the remainder of this section covering techniques designed to encourage behaviors, I am including Natural Consequences and Created Consequences, although these techniques can just as easily be used to discourage behaviors. The reason for this is that I prefer that you get into the habit of thinking in terms of how to positively use consequences to encourage behavior, since consequences are sometimes mistakenly thought of—and used as—punishment.

Natural Consequences

Consider letting the powerful impact of natural consequences shape your child's behavior wherever possible. To do so results in him learning something important, improves his behavior, and contributes to his overall development. Natural consequences occur as a result of action taken and are hard to argue with, resist or ignore—and the main reason for this being one of my favorite techniques. Parental intervention or involvement, on the other hand, can be argued with, resisted, and ignored. When you let natural consequences impact his poor behavior (as in when he frequently hits other children, they no longer include him in their play and he experiences loneliness), he is faced with managing a reality he cannot change. If he chooses not to change his behavior, he must experience the consequence of his choice (loneliness). If he chooses to change his behavior, he avoids being lonely and is instead faced with an opportunity to join in the play and have fun. One can assume that he would rather have fun than be left out and feel lonely. The consequence helps him learn how to behave kindly towards others. Here are some pointers that might help when preparing to use this technique:

- Select a behavior that will not make your child experience too much frustration or discomfort when he experiences the consequences. You must be able to resist jumping in and rescuing him for this approach to work.

- Make sure there is a direct and obvious connection between his behavior and the resultant consequence so that he actually feels its impact.

Example of a Natural Consequence: your child habitually forgets his coat and lunch when leaving for school and you want to encourage his independence and remember for himself. However, you have spoken to him about it numerous times and nothing has changed. You either run after him before he gets on the bus, or drive to school with the coat and lunch. He is in second grade and absolutely capable of taking care of these things himself, but he does not have to give it a second thought because you are doing all the work for him. If you can stand to let him go cold and hungry for a day or two, do so. (If you do not want to let him to suffer the natural consequences of his behavior, you could try a different technique such as Positive Reinforcement for each time he remembers to take his coat and lunch.) Tell him that he is mature enough and perfectly capable of re-membering his coat and lunch from now on and that you will no longer be delivering forgotten items. You may remind him *once* if it makes you feel better, but you do not have to. He knows the routine. When he leaves his coat and lunch at home next time, do not take them to school. He will experience some discomfort if he has to go out in the cold, or if his stomach growls all afternoon, but he will not suffer any lasting damage. However, he *will* remember to take his coat and lunch next time. By letting him experience the natural consequences of his forgetfulness, you have let him take another important developmental step: how to take care of him-self. (Note: You may want to get his teacher's or the school's support ahead of time, particularly if they have previously involved you when he has forgotten these items.)

Created Consequences

Sometimes you must create a consequence to help shape your child's be-havior because there is no natural consequence available that will prompt him to make a positive change. The purpose and goal of the technique is the same as it is with Natural Consequences—that is to help him do some-thing for himself, encourage his independence and contribute to his over-all development. Use the same decision criteria outlined in the Natural Consequences section when selecting which behavior to impact.

Example of a Created Consequence that encourages behavior: Your eight-year-old loves to play at his friend's house, but he strongly resists coming home. No matter what you have planned for the rest of the day, he does not want to leave and puts up a fight every time you arrive to pick him up. Much to your dismay, he has also started to use offensive language. You demand that he come in a firm voice, but he has learned that your firm voice carries little weight. He has learned that nothing happens when he ignores your request, or whines at you to change it. Today you threaten to withdraw the privilege of playing at his friend's house for a week, but he regards this as an empty threat. He knows you are reluctant to punish his friend along with him. Instead of possibly painting yourself into a corner, you can create a consequence and let him experience its impact. Here's how:

Tell him that the next time he refuses to come home at the agreed-upon time, you will interpret that as an indication he is over-tired. Because of that, he will have to go straight to his bedroom when he gets home and stay there for the remainder of the day in order to catch up on his rest. Be prepared to bear the brunt of his anger towards you if you must let the consequence take effect. A child's anger can be intimidating to a parent, and an effective way to compel you to give in. However, I urge you to hold firm—for his sake. He is testing the limits you have set to see if you will hold firm, and his expression of anger (though perhaps not in the best way), is not an abnormal way to react. Rest assured you are helping him develop the essential social skills of anger management and emotional containment.

Example of a Created Consequence that discourages behavior: Your child plays video games or watches television almost to the exclusion of doing anything else with his free time. You do not want to stop the behavior altogether, but you do want to reduce the amount of time he engages in it. The quickest and most effective approach is to regulate access to and use of the controller for either the video games or television. Although this may seem a simple approach, few parents actually use it. Instead, in an effort to encourage their child to make his own decisions and regulate his own behavior, many parents make arrangements that leave the decision to the child. Temptation eventually takes over, resulting in an increase in the behavior again. This pattern usually repeats itself until it causes conflict between parent and child. A respectful way to deal with this problem is to make an agreement with your child about when, and for how long, he can play the games or watch television, then take control of the remotes so that he has access to them only at the arranged times.

Techniques that Discourage Behavior

Although it is important to discourage certain behaviors—and the 12 techniques that follow in this section will help you do this—it is just as important while doing so to focus on the fact that you are simultaneously trying to encourage others. For example, when using The Bag technique, not only are you discouraging your child from being untidy, but you are also encouraging him to be neat and to be respectful of his and others' possessions. When using the Time Out or Quiet Place techniques, not only are you stopping unruly or reckless behavior, but you are also encouraging the development of your child's ability to contain himself. His misbehaving provides you with an opportunity to redirect the energy towards healthy behaving. Looking at discipline in this light helps you remain positive while helping your child change his behaviors.

The Bag

When used in the right way, this method of encouraging your child to tidy up his toys, and other possessions is a real winner. I would suggest that you use a large, black trash bag, or something similar that can hold a large number of toys for a few days. You can use this technique on a child from about the age of three, but not much before that.

Example: You are tired of walking through toys and other messes at the end of each day and decide it is time for your child to do some of his own picking up. First, spend a day or two looking at which toys he plays with most and either put the rest in storage or give them away. Keep the number of toys available to a minimum. When you are ready, choose a time when he is in a receptive mood, and casually let him know what you are planning, and why. As usual, customize the following example in your own words, but keep the message the same:

"Kenny, I think you're old enough to start picking up your toys, so here's something I'd like you to try. Just before your bath, take a little time to tidy up. Things that aren't put away will go into this bag until Saturday and then you can have them back." (Note: The only things that do not go in the bag are his favorite bed toy, or school things.) Answer any questions he may have and then drop the subject since you have already explained what you are doing and why. At the designated time, remind him that it is time to pick up his toys— and when it is done, time for bath, play or books with you, and bed. At bath time, go ahead as normal.

Outcome #1: He puts his things away before bath time. Wonderful! Tell him what a great job he did.

Outcome #2: He does not put his things away before bath time. Say nothing about the mess. Proceed to the bath and the rest of the evening as usual. If he forgets to do it before his bath, but puts things away afterwards, that is okay. The toys are put away and only the things left out go in the bag. Ask if he would rather do it at that time tomorrow night too, or put them away before his bath, and go with his decision.

Outcome #3: He puts nothing away either before or after his bath. If he brings up the subject before bed, simply remind him that he can try again the next evening before his bath. When he is in bed, put all the toys he did not put away in the bag and leave it out of his sight until Saturday. If he notices some things are missing the next day, remind him about the new deal and that he can get his things back on Saturday. Repeat this process each night until Saturday morning. On Saturday, give him the bag and let him put his toys away. What he does not put away goes back in the bag that night and stays in the bag until the following Saturday. The good thing about this system is that, over time, you whittle down the amount of toys he neither plays with nor cares for. After a few weeks you should no longer need the bag, there will be fewer toys to deal with, and what is left will be put away. Problem solved!

Time Out

The Time Out technique is *not a punishment*, but is designed to help your child contain himself when he is physically or emotionally out of control. It is best used to eliminate dangerous and aggressive behaviors, or extremely inconvenient or annoying behaviors, that have not responded to correction by use of another technique. Do not use Time Out as the first—or default—technique for every behavior. Use it judiciously. If used correctly and for the right behavior, Time Out should produce an immediate reduction in the number of times he misbehaves. If you are using it for the right behavior and you see no change, review the setup and implementation steps below and make sure you are following the process closely.

For Time Out to be effective, you must temporarily deprive your child of your attention. When he is too young for a real Time Out, simply turning your back on him (Time Out for Toddlers), will deliver the message. That should be enough. Time Out can be used on children from about age two and a half and up. After age eight or nine, most children have developed the ability to contain themselves. If they have not developed that ability, consider using another technique, such as the Quiet Place.

When you decide to use Time Out, follow the process below as you prepare. The setup step is crucial for a successful outcome, so it is worth spending time on.

The Setup

- Make sure you and your partner agree on which behavior you want to eliminate. Select just one behavior, until you are satisfied with the outcome, and then try it on another.

- Pick a spot in the home that you will always use for Time Out. Keep a child between the ages of two and a half and four where he can see you and you can keep an eye on him. An older child can either be in or out of your sight, as long as you can tell whether or not he has calmed down.

- Develop the message you will use when you tell him what behaviors will earn a Time Out. Keep it simple, clear and *short.* For example, "Jon, your dad and I don't want you to (hit, kick, fill in the blank) anymore. It hurts people when you do that and we won't allow that kind of behavior. When you do it again, you will have to go to Time Out." (Note that the word "when" is used instead of "if," because you *know* he will do it again.) "We will let you out of Time Out once you have sat there calmly and quietly for a while." Answer any questions he may have to make sure he gets the message but do not get drawn into a discussion, bargaining, or deal making.

- Deliver the message. This must be a time when he is *not* engaged in the unwanted behavior and when he is not tired, hungry, cranky, or otherwise upset.

- Prepare yourself for delivering the message. Although you may be upset or irritated with him, put those feelings aside and keep your voice and tone light, sincere and confident. Now you are ready to use the Time Out technique.

Implementing Time Out

- When he engages in the unwanted behavior, do not give any warnings, but simply repeat the message you delivered during the setup as you put him in Time Out. Do not enter into discussion with him, and remind him that you will let him know when he can come out.

- Do not set a timer or give him a predetermined length of time to sit there. His behavior determines how long he stays in Time Out. He gets out when he has been calm and quiet (with no intervention from you) for thirty seconds (two and a half to four years), or one minute (four years and up). The count does not start until he stops whining, crying, begging, or getting out of Time Out. If he does get out before it is time, firmly put him back without talking. If you must talk, simply repeat your message, nothing more. Repeat this until he stays there, remaining calm and quiet, for the required length of time.

- When he has been calm and quiet for the required length of time, tell him he can come out. Then go about your business as usual, making no mention of why he was in Time Out—he knows why he had to go and now is not the time for either of you to argue about it. If you need to discuss how he can behave better, by all means do so, but not when he has just come out of Time Out. If you consistently engage him in conversation about his behavior immediately after Time Out, he may use getting sent to Time Out as a means to get your attention.

If he goes to Time Out willingly and never fusses when there, he probably does not need it. If you think his behavior still needs reinforcement, try another technique instead. When Time Out fails to work

and the misbehavior continues, consider the following possible causes:
- He is too young to understand what is going on or why he is there.
- He enjoys the attention of being in—and being let out of—Time Out because you engage with him during those times.
- It was the wrong choice of technique.
- You are using it inconsistently.
- He needs to be taught some alternate ways of behaving.

If it is the right choice of technique and you are applying it correctly and consistently, it *will* work.

Time Out in Public

Use the Time Out in Public when your child throws a tantrum, is disruptive in a restaurant or store, runs away from you, otherwise loses control of himself, and misbehaves in public. When he behaves in these ways, he runs the risk of being embarrassed or ashamed—or could pose a danger to himself or others—and it is best to help him avoid any of these situations for the sake of his developing self-esteem, as well as for his safety. Perhaps disciplining him in public will make you feel embarrassed or ashamed when other people stare at you, but he needs you to take the lead as the adult and parent.

- Follow the steps described in the Setup of the previous Time Out section. Decide what you will say when you tell him what behavior you will not tolerate in public, and why. Then explain what will happen if he transgresses.

Implementing Time Out in Public

- Take him to a restroom if you are in a restaurant or store or to your car if you prefer (or if that is the only choice.) Let him know you will stay there until he calms down, and that you will return to what you were doing when he is calm.

• Wait with him in the restroom or the car and resist being drawn into discussion or negotiation with him. You can calmly tell him— repeatedly, if necessary—that when he is calm and quiet you will take him back. If you are feeling frustrated or irritated with his behavior, feel compassion for him. After all, he is in distress and needs your patient help. When he has been calm and quiet for thirty seconds or a minute (depending on his age as noted in the Implementing Time Out section above), ask him if he is ready to return. If so, thank him for being calm and take him back with no mention of his behavior. He knows why he was in Time Out— you can discuss alternative ways of behaving at a later time, not immediately after Time Out.

Time Out in a Moving Car

Prepare your child ahead of time if you possibly can so that he knows what will happen if he gets out of control in the car. Explain that it is necessary for everyone's safety and that you will pull over and wait until he is calm before moving again. The next time he is disruptive in the car, pull over to the side of the road *in a safe place* as soon as possible. Tell him you will wait quietly and continue once he has stopped being disruptive and has calmed down enough for you to drive safely. Then wait him out. There is no need for you to talk or answer questions or concerns about arriving late. Even if you are concerned about arriving late, remember that driving with a disruptive child is dangerous and is not worth an accident. If you feel you must say something, remind him only that you will continue when he has calmed down enough for you to drive. *You* determine when he is calm enough, so ignore any pleading to continue driving. He will eventually settle down. When he does, you can thank him for doing so and continue driving to your destination—without reference to his behavior.

Time Out with a Toddler

A child younger than two or two and a half is too young to understand the implications of Time Out, but sometimes his behavior warrants immediate containment when redirecting him is ineffective. Such containment is necessary when he is aggressive, out of control, or putting himself in harm's way.

Since Time Out works best when you temporarily deprive him of your attention, the best way to do this with a toddler is to firmly but calmly tell him "No hitting/biting, etc." put him down if you are holding him, and turn your back on him. Use of both verbal and non-verbal signals gives weight to your message. Although all the following scenarios require that you turn your back, always keep an "eye" on him for his safety.

- If he is confined to a high-chair, this is easy. Simply turn away from him to convey the message that his behavior is not going to be noticed. As soon as he returns to normal behavior, turn around and engage positively with him.

- If he is not confined and tends to run off when you tell him "No hitting," pick him up, take him with you into a confined space or small room, and put him gently down as you say "No hitting." Turn your back, wait until he returns to normal, then turn around and engage positively with him.

- If he does not run off and is content to stay near you, tell him "No hitting," turn your back on him, and go about your business as he trails after you. Positively acknowledge him once he is calm.

- If you are in public, take him to the car or off to the side of the activity, tell him "No hitting," and stay with him (restrained in his seat if in the car) until he is calm. Then engage positively with him as you take him back to where you were.

It is important to immediately give him the message when he misbehaves, turn away from him, and then immediately give him positive attention once he has returned to his normal self. If your responses are not immediate, he will not make the connection between his misbehavior and your correction, or his good behavior and your positive attention. There is no point in telling him that he should not behave that way, giving him a lecture, or explaining things to him. Your actions speak much more loudly—and effectively— than your words.

The Quiet Place

In his book *Children Are from Heaven*, John Gray, PhD, writes about a behavioral technique that can be used with children from about the age of three and up with great effect. The technique I use is similar to Dr. Gray's, and I call it The Quiet Place.

The Quiet Place is similar to the Time Out technique in that it is used to give your child a safe and comfortable place to calm down and contain himself. It can be extremely useful when he is really angry with a sibling (or you) or when you have tried everything else to get him to calm down and he remains out of control. It is an alternative to Time Out for an older child, or if your child prefers to be removed from the activity rather than feel exposed in Time Out.

The Quiet Place is a spot he creates for himself; ideally it should be in his bedroom. He can fill it with his favorite things to make it special. It is his alone to enter—nobody goes in uninvited. He can name it whatever he wants, and that is the name other people call it. As with Time Out, I want to stress this technique should not be seen as a punishment. It is merely a means for you to respectfully let him contain his emotions and behaviors.

The Setup

- As with Time Out, determine which behavior warrants the Quiet Place. Have him prepare his spot, with your help if requested.
- Prepare the message you will deliver to him that explains why he must go to the Quiet Place. For example, "John, when you hurt your brother or get totally out of control, screaming and throwing things, you can go to your Quiet Place to calm down. After you've been quiet for a short while, I'll invite you to come out, but I won't let you open the door and I won't talk to you while you're in there."
- Answer any questions he has, but do not argue or negotiate.

Implement the Quiet Place

Sometimes he may actually take himself to his Quiet Place once he realizes how helpful it can be. Encourage that. If he does not go voluntarily, take him when he needs to go, and close the door securely. Hold it closed if necessary and do not engage with him in any way. Do this until he calms down completely, and then invite him out. It may take him a while to thoroughly burn out his frustration and calm down. He may reach a crescendo of screaming or crying, but it is important to let him experience the whole process and not interrupt, no matter how much he begs. His distress can be alarming and tough to listen to, especially the pleading. Just remember that you are doing him a great favor by letting him experience—and then contain—his emotions independently. He is taking an important developmental step. When he comes out, give him affection if *he* initiates it. Otherwise, just go about things as normal. He "did the crime and paid the time" so he's off the hook!

Control the Environment

The concept of controlling your child's environment sounds like a fairly simple one, but it takes some inventive thought to do it well. However, once you learn how and when to use this technique, you can avoid getting into power struggles and feeding the development of unwanted behaviors. Controlling the environment enables you to be proactive and avoid using the word "no" thus giving your child fewer opportunities to defy you.

You probably started to control his environment back when he was in the crawling stage by child-proofing your home, preventing him from getting into trouble with drawers, cupboards, and light sockets. As he ages, you will have to make appropriate changes to the nature of control.

Example #1: Your child tends to climb up on the dining table and has fallen off a couple of times. Luckily, you caught him each time, but he will not stop. You can control his environment by simply moving the chairs away from the table, thus removing his makeshift ladder.

Example #2: He prefers to ride his bike without a helmet and you find yourself fighting with him to wear one. Control the environment by putting his bike where he cannot get to it and only letting him have it when he has his helmet on. Do not argue with him, but remind him *once* that when he has his helmet on, you will get the bike. Say nothing, but wait because sooner or later he will get the message that no helmet = no bike. If he wants to ride badly enough, he will wear his helmet.

Example #3: Perhaps he snacks constantly but rarely eats a full meal. It bothers you that he might not be getting the proper nutrition. Wisely wanting to avoid a fight over food and eating, control the environment by only buying—and giving him access to—the kind of foods you want him to eat. Only allow a maximum of two small snacks per day (one of which might only be a drink, not something to eat). At mealtimes, give him what the rest of the family is eating. If he chooses not to eat the meal, do not give him something else that he prefers. Instead let his natural hunger shape his behavior. He will eat well at the next meal. If you need to, use the End of Picky Eating technique to encourage better eating habits.

Making use of appropriate parental control to prevent problems is a great way to minimize the conflicts in your home.

Active Ignoring

Although I have seen others use this technique, and have used it many times myself with great results, I have never heard a name given to it, so I call it the Active Ignoring technique. The reason I call it *Active* Ignoring is because there is a difference between ignoring and *actively* ignoring, just as there is a difference between listening and *actively* listening. When you ignore someone, you simply do not listen to them; you tune them out. When you *actively* ignore someone, deliberately and obviously, it conveys the message that you are *choosing* not to respond to what they are doing or saying. Admittedly, it is somewhat counter-intuitive for parents to ignore their children. If this is so with you, I urge you to recall the sailboat metaphor from Chapter 5 in the Power Struggle Behaviors section that describes how attention from you at the wrong time can act as "wind" to your child's "sails" (resistance) and involve you both in a power struggle. Rest assured your attitude of non-response is for his benefit. Prior to using this technique, let him know that you will not respond to specific behaviors. Be sure he understands which behaviors you will do this with. The next time he engages in that behavior, or behaviors, let him know you will not respond. And then don't. When he is through behaving in that particular way, engage positively with him.

Example: You are at the movies buying tickets and told him before arriving that you would not be buying any candy or soda. You also told him that if he asks for anything, you will ignore his requests because you want him to learn to listen to what you say. As soon as the tickets are paid for, he starts to insist that he have candy or popcorn and soda. Immediately you remember to use the Active Ignoring technique, you remind him you are going to ignore him, then do not respond to his pleas.

Outcome #1: He remembers what you told him and quiets down. Talk positively to him about the movie you are about to see, or something else.

Outcome #2: He continues to ask, then begins to whine, beg and plead. Actively ignoring him does not seem to be working. You may remind him once that you are choosing not to respond to his pleas because you have already told him you are not buying anything at the cinema tonight. If he continues, however, you may have to use Time Out in Public in order to stop the behavior, inconvenient though it may be. At this point, if you fail to follow through as planned, he will push you harder next time he wants something because you have given him the message that you do not mean what you say.

The End of Picky Eating

This technique is the only one I know of that works to put an end to your child's picky eating habits, but be warned: it is one that relies on him being allowed to feel his hunger. A child experiencing normal growth needs to eat a regular meal shortly after getting up, sometime during the middle of the day, and at the end of the day. In between he can have two small snacks of something nutritious such as fruit, and a drink that is not loaded with sugar. Other than that, all he really needs is water to keep hydrated throughout the day.

If your child is showing signs of poor or picky eating habits, you might consider helping him change them now, rather than waiting until the habits get worse as he grows into late childhood and early adolescence. Identify his (and your) habits first (for a review of problematic eating styles, turn back to Picky or Poor Eating Behaviors in Chapter 5, page 114.) Is he an Interrupter, a Grazer, or a Selector? Are you a Chef, a Persuader, or a Preacher? Once you have identified your and your child's habits, you may be ready to consider making a change. This technique, like setting limits or expectations, involves a Setup step and a Follow-through step.

The Setup

- Get prepared mentally to let your child experience hunger if he chooses not to eat.
- When you are ready, decide when you will make the change, and prepare the message you will deliver to let everyone know your plan. Keep it simple and clear: "I'm going to start something different tomorrow, and want to give you a heads up. From now on I would like everyone to eat what I prepare—no substitutions. If there is something being served you don't like, you don't have to eat it, but there won't be any other choices either. If you get down from the table to play, that will tell me you have finished and I will clear your plate away. In between meals you can have your normal snacks.
- Answer any questions that come up, and make any other preparations you deem necessary.

The Follow Through

Start the new regime at the pre-arranged time and tell the family the meal is ready. All you need to do now is to follow through with your part of the arrangement—that is to serve everyone what you have prepared with no substitutions when they complain or refuse to eat it. Whether you are a Chef, a Persuader or a Preacher, refrain from falling into your old habits and simply stick to the message you delivered in the Setup.

Outcome #1: Everyone falls in with the new arrangement, finishes their meal, clears up and goes about their day. It could happen, but don't hold your breath!

Outcome #2: Your child starts his meal, runs off to play and you remove his plate. He returns and loudly complains about his food being gone. Remind him that his behavior told you he was finished and he can eat again at the next meal. Do not respond to his complaints or whining as you finish your meal, or supplement his hunger with larger than normal snacks before the next meal. Repeat this until he stays at the table through an entire meal.

Outcome #3: Your child says he does not like the pasta, the cheese, or the tomatoes and wants a peanut butter and jelly sandwich. You remind him that there are no substitutions and he can eat his food or wait until the next meal. If he continues to complain you can remove his plate and tell him he can leave the table, or tune him out as you finish your meal. Do not supplement his hunger with larger than normal snacks before the next meal. Repeat this until he develops healthy eating behaviors.

Withdraw From the Fight

This technique poses a challenge for some parents—and might be difficult for you too, because withdrawing from a fight or a power struggle with your child requires you to relinquish a certain amount of control. You might think that if *you* are not in control, things will get out of control. If so, pick an issue that you can walk away from without discomfort. Essentially, by using this technique, you are choosing to no longer enable your child's inappropriate behavior, but are instead allowing him to learn from the consequences of his behavior.

Example #1: Your eight-year-old does not put his dirty clothes in the hamper, although you have asked him to do so a million times. Usually you go into his room, pick up the dirty clothes and wash them. This indicates to him that it is your job, not his, so he does not have to do anything.

Instead, give him fair warning when you are planning to do laundry, and tell him that you will wash whatever he has put in the hamper by then. When it is time to do laundry and his clothes are not in the hamper, do not pick them up and wash them. Do not give little (or big) hints! If the clothes are scattered about the house and getting in the way, put them in a pile by his bed or dresser. Eventually he will bring up the subject. When he does, remind him that you will let him know the next time you are doing laundry and will wash whatever is in the hamper at that time.

If you find it hard to refrain from asking, reminding or hinting, you may have difficulty at first with this technique and feel that picking up the clothes and washing them is so much easier than the alternative. And it is—until you get fed up with the old way and start the nagging again. Real change will only come about when you stop the enabling by doing things that you have asked him to do—and is capable of doing. If he does put his clothes in the hamper, thank him for doing so. Sooner or later the natural consequence of not having an item, or items, he needs, will prompt him to comply with your request. You will have to be prepared for him to wear— and others to see—crumpled or dirty clothes. If you are unwilling to allow this, use another technique such as setting an expectation with Positive Reinforcement for his compliance.

Example #2: Your nine-year-old son consistently "forgets" to pick up his room on Saturday morning, even though he has agreed to do it at that time. The more he has resisted, the more you have nagged, and things are now at an uncomfortable impasse. What are your choices? You could withdraw a privilege or ground him, but there is a high probability that either consequence will result in building, or increasing, resentment between the two of you. Withdrawing from the fight might be a more effective option. Start by telling him, "I'm sure you're as tired as I am of fighting over tidying your room on Saturday morning. We both know you *can* do it, but for some reason you *don't* do it. I don't think it's worth the fight any more so I'm just going to let you decide what you're going to do. One thing I ask is that you keep your bedroom door shut so I can't see the mess." You will never have to go in there unless you choose. If you normally leave his clean laundry in his room, leave it somewhere else that is not in your way. If he cleans his room, he will eventually let you know. Until he does, assume it is still a mess and stay out.

Perhaps you cannot live with the fact that he might never clean his room. If that is the case, set an expectation (with a Created consequence) that his room is to be cleaned before lunch. When lunch time comes around and his room is clean, congratulate him on his success. When he comes in for lunch and his room is not cleaned, remind him he can have lunch if he has cleaned it in time. If he cleans the room and lunch is over, tell him he has missed lunch, but if he cleans it before supper, he can join you then. If he still has not cleaned his room by supper, or by the time supper is over, tell him he can have breakfast if he has cleaned it by then. You will not have to keep this up very long if you follow through with what you say, because the natural consequence of his hunger will motivate him to comply.

Withdrawing Privileges

Although I know many parents are familiar with, and like to use, this technique, it is not one of my favorites because it is hard to identify just what is, and what is not, a privilege. For example, is it a privilege for your child to watch television, have a friend over, or go on a family outing? Or are those things his right because he is a member of the family? If a privilege cannot be defined or given, then it cannot be taken away. Only use this technique if you first clearly define what a privilege is, and then withdraw it for clearly defined infractions. When you become angry with him, it is easy to fly off the handle and say, "If you don't do such-and-such, you won't be able to watch television for a week!" But are you really going to monitor that with your busy lifestyle? Are you going to be around to enforce it? Even if you do remember, and can enforce it, there may be a fight every time you try. It is possible that he will let you take things away, just to see how far you will go. I have seen parents take away everything they can and it still does not change the behavior because the child continues to hold out as his resentment builds. Using a technique such as Natural or Created consequences will prove more effective and prevent an unpleasant buildup of resentment. Always look for a way to positively reinforce his good behaviors before resorting to punishment.

Grounding

Although many of the techniques described in this chapter are aimed at helping young children change their behaviors, parents of an older child might choose to use grounding as an alternative. It works best with those who are independent enough to spend time away from home with friends, sometime after the age of eleven, and can be used effectively with teenagers too. But, as with the Withdrawing Privileges technique, it must be used sparingly and appropriately to be effective, and you must be prepared to enforce it. Decide ahead of time which behaviors will merit grounding (and for how long), otherwise it is too easy to get caught up in the heat of the moment. You may suddenly blurt out, "You're grounded for three months!" and then find enforcing it impossible. This kind of mistake is hard to correct once the words are out of your mouth. Grounding is best when it fits the crime—that is, when your older child or teen repeatedly fails to return home at the agreed-upon time (assuming that transportation is not an issue). It should not be used for poor grades, for answering back and annoying you, or for such things as foul language. Although you may want to ground your child for any of these behaviors, it is not an appropriate technique to use. Here are some alternative suggestions: Active Listening, Natural or Created consequences, and Positive Reinforcement. All of these approaches are good for improving the relationship whereas grounding—when inappropriately used—can be destructive. However, if you are prepared and ready to use grounding because you believe it is a good fit for the behavior, follow these suggestions:

- Beforehand, clearly tell your child what behavior or behaviors will merit grounding and be sure there is no misunderstanding. Also tell him how long the grounding will last and what being grounded means, and stick to it. Does it mean being confined to home and school only? Does it allow for visits with family but not friends? Does it allow for visits to certain friends and not others? You can see how difficult it is to actually set up properly, but if you do not, it will not work.

- As to length of time, I would suggest a timeframe between two days and one week, depending on the severity of the behavior. Anything less than two days will not have enough of an impact. Anything longer than one week is overkill, will lessen the impact, and will lead to the backfiring and resentment mentioned above.

- When your child transgresses, there is no need to warn him. Simply remind him which behaviors merit grounding and for how long, start the clock, and let him know exactly when the grounding will be over. Then stick to it. Do not prolong the grounding beyond the agreed-upon length of time, even if he misbehaves again during the grounding period. I have seen some groundings endlessly lengthened, and the child—not surprisingly—finally gives up trying to cooperate. If he is not affected by grounding and repeatedly gets in more trouble while grounded, this may be proof that you have selected the wrong technique and consider using Setting Limits, or Setting Expectations with Natural or Created consequences as a follow-through.

- Do not get drawn into negotiations while he is grounded or when he gets out. He has fulfilled his side of the agreement and it is time to move forward.

As you can see from reading the material in this chapter, there are a variety of techniques to encourage or discourage your child's behaviors. Try out different ones—over time you will find those that work best for you and he. You will probably find your favorites and end up using only two or three. When you use a new technique, follow the instructions as closely as possible, and adapt them to fit the relationship you have with your child, your lifestyle and circumstances. Whenever you have success with a particular technique, help other parents by showing them how and when to use it. Your family and theirs will be happy you shared.

CHAPTER 8

ESTABLISHING HEALTHY ROUTINES

B efore deciding to establish a routine, it is best if you have first had time to practice and develop confidence in how to set limits and expectations, as well as having used some other behavioral techniques. By doing this you will have developed the confidence you will need when you decide to establish a routine. The more effectively you establish routines, the more your life will run like a well-oiled machine; and the more preparation you put in beforehand, the more successful you will be. A routine is made up of a series of expectations about which behaviors should be performed by whom over a defined period of time. Setting up and establishing a routine requires that you and your partner identify a series of sequential steps for everyone to follow and reward compliance with Positive Reinforcement. If one step is not completed fully, or at all, simply give your child a brief reminder and move on to the next step in the routine. Not following the established routine will result in her being deprived of something at some point in the process. By now you should be familiar with using both Natural and Created consequences, so allowing them to have an impact will ensure her compliance after a few tries.

The wonderful thing about established and effective routines is that you can be on autopilot and not have to think about, worry about, or get frustrated over every little thing that must be accomplished. Routines create a satisfying atmosphere for everyone, especially the children. And this phenomenon is not confined to family life, since routines create the same sense of satisfaction in the business world too.

Research has shown that companies that identify which processes (or routines) to implement, and then implement them, have a higher rate of satisfaction among employees, are more profitable, and become more solidly successful than their counterparts that are not as process oriented. Families benefit in the same way.

As with many of the techniques covered in this book, there is a setup step and a follow-through step to establishing routines. The rest of this section addresses a few of the most popular routines, and below are some steps you can follow in preparation to setting them up:

- With your partner, pick the routine you would like to establish and name it.
- Identify the routine's boundaries (when it starts and ends) and identify its basic steps.
- Discuss your ideas with the children to get buy-in and outline the steps of the routine.
- Try out the routine for a while, adjust anything that is not working, and then try out the new and improved version. Keep adjusting parts of the routine as necessary until it is working like clockwork most of the time.
- Reinforce the routine until it becomes a habit.

The Morning Routine

In most families, mornings are hectic, especially on school and workdays when there is a lot to do in a small amount of time. Here are some suggestions that can make mornings a little less stressful:

- Select and name the routine: morning routine.
- Identify routine boundaries: between waking up and leaving the house for school or work.

- Identify the basic steps: get up, take a shower, dress, brush teeth, eat, prepare what you need to take with you, and leave the house at a certain time.

The most important part of setting up a routine is to get the family together for a working meeting. The goal is to get everyone's buy-in, along with a clear understanding of what each person will be required to do at each step. Tell the children when the routine begins and ends, and the basic steps you have identified. Ask for their ideas about how they can get each step done. Keep a simple outline of what each person has said they will do, and make sure it is realistic. The more input you get from the children, the more likely they will be willing to carry out their parts of the routine.

Do not be concerned about getting everything right until you have all had some time (about a week) to try it out. Inject as much creativity and humor into the process as possible since that seems to be more effective. If you are deadly serious about getting it right, doing it perfectly, and expecting too much, you will never get to the point of implementing the routine. It will seem like too much work. Rehearsing gives everyone the opportunity to iron out the kinks before there is a good working version. Get feedback from everybody about how things are going, and how they might be improved. Once you have been through the rehearsal period and think you have the worst of the kinks ironed out, see how things go for a few days. If there are any problems with compliance after this point, you can start implementing reinforcements as you see fit. Some techniques I would suggest are: Active Listening, Positive Reinforcement, and Natural or Created consequences.

The most common problem with the morning routine is that your child does not get up, get dressed, or eat in time to leave, and holds everyone up. Since she has already had ample time to give her input and rehearse what to do, here are some options for handling the problem:

- Get her up ten minutes earlier the first day after the routine has been broken. If that does not work, get her up twenty minutes earlier the next day. Keep this up until she has enough time to get ready. Either she will protest and speed up, thus reclaiming the sleep time taken from her, or she really does need the extra time.

- If you drive her to school, let her know five minutes before it is time to leave. If necessary, help her gather everything together and get in the car, whether or not she has finished dressing or eating breakfast. Bring whatever clothes she has not put on into the car and she can finish dressing in the car before you leave. The natural consequence of either arriving late at school or not eating breakfast will motivate her to get with the program the next day. If she has also forgotten her lunch, she will suffer the consequence of further hunger.

- If she carpools or takes the bus but misses her ride, you will have to take her by car. Follow the suggestions in the preceding paragraph.

Another problem commonly encountered during the morning routine is that your child may be reluctant to brush her teeth. Let her know that her teeth are not protected when they have not been cleaned, so she cannot have anything containing refined sugar to eat or drink for breakfast such as cereal, bread, jelly, or fruit juice. Food constraints such as these essentially mean she will have a limited selection from which to choose, since most traditional breakfast foods are loaded with sugar. She will change her mind about brushing if you stick to your guns and give her something without refined sugar for as long as her teeth remain un-brushed.

After school routine

- Select and name the routine: after school routine
- Identify routine boundaries: between the end of school and dinner.
- Identify the basic steps: after school sports, classes, practice, and homework.

Go through the routine setup process, as you did with the morning routine and try out the first version of your after school routine.

Problems encountered during the after school routine revolve around collecting the necessary clothing and equipment for activities, and getting homework done. When you are working out the details with the family about this routine, be sure everyone is clear about when, and what, things need to be ready for each activity and help them get prepared until they can do it themselves. Perhaps having everything together in one spot (even in the car trunk) would be a convenient way to manage things at first.

Leave on time for all activities and expect your child to have everything she needs. If she does not, she will soon learn if you allow her to experience the consequences of her lack of readiness. If she arrives late, let her experience whatever the consequences of tardiness are. If she continues to be late, perhaps she does not want to continue the activity and you will have to consider stopping it. If you somehow hold her accountable, it will not take long to learn, but it may be somewhat inconvenient for everyone concerned. Resist the temptation to do it all for her, although it may be much more convenient in the short term.

Allow plenty of time for her to complete her homework. If she is not done in time, move on to the next step of the routine leaving her to figure out how and when to complete it—or let her go to school with incomplete work. Letting your child struggle over homework can be hard for any parent, so figure out your comfort level and tell her teacher what you are trying to do to support her independence. Since homework can be so disruptive to the after school routine, it is addressed in its own section below.

Homework

Some children do their homework without ever needing encouragement. They enjoy schoolwork and enjoy homework just as much. But, this is not the case with all children. Some find school difficult, some struggle over certain subjects, and others are neutral about the whole affair. Whether or not your child does her homework willingly depends on her school experience, how well she understands the material, how much she likes her teachers, and how happy she is with life in general.

If she resists doing homework, take time to find out why. If she is truly struggling with the subject matter, arrange extra help at school until she is up to speed. If something upsetting is going on in her life—such as a move from one school to another, problems with friends, or a distressing family matter—attend to her needs before expecting her to concentrate on doing homework.

If you fight with her over homework every day, ask her teacher for input. Let him or her know you are trying some things at home, and that you are in full support of whatever consequences or policies are in place at school to manage this problem. In this way, you and the teacher will be reinforcing and supporting one another's expectations. Wherever possible, keep out of the homework dilemma yourself, and let your child and her teacher work together to resolve any issues. If you suspect she is resisting doing homework because she dislikes doing anything at home that is school related, or she is resisting what she sees as your nagging, withdraw from the power struggle and see if that helps.

Example: "You and I have been fighting too much over you doing your homework. I really don't like doing that, and I'm sure you don't like it either.

178

Since you've told me you don't have any trouble doing your work, there's not really any need for me to be involved, unless you ask for my help. I think you're capable of doing it on your own, and I don't want to get in the way. So from now on, I'm going to let you do it on your own. You can remind me to stay out of it if I start bugging you again!"

Once you have had a conversation with her and have her understanding and agreement as to why she must complete her homework, step back and let her do it—or not—on her own. There may be some fallout at school, if she hands in inferior work. If so, let her experience the natural consequences of whatever the school's policy dictates. Of course, praise her when she completes her homework and only check it if she asks you to.

I expect you, like most parents, feel pressured to do all you can to help your child succeed in school. But if you get too involved at an early age, she will never learn from her mistakes, nor will she feel the accomplishment of handing in her own (perhaps imperfect) work. Stay out of this activity as much as you possibly can if you want her to develop good study habits. Over-involvement on your part can give her the message that she is inadequate and incapable of doing the work alone. It can also lead to laziness if she sees that you are willing to do it for her. So think long and hard before you get involved and keep that involvement to an absolute minimum. An important part of learning and excelling is failing.

Wherever possible use a Natural consequence to motivate your child to complete her homework before using another technique such as a Created consequence. Occasionally add in some Positive Reinforcement; do something special, but simple, you know she enjoys. However, do not tell her ahead of time that you will do something fun if she completes her homework, because she will smell a bribe.

If you have refrained from getting involved with homework, and if you have let consequences at school reinforce the message that the homework must be done, *and* if you have added Positive Reinforcement . . . and she *still* is not doing homework on her own, you indeed may need to create a powerful consequence. Give her plenty of time to succeed on her own first, though, because it may take a while for her to turn things around.

Coming up with a suitable Created consequence may challenge your imagination as well as possibly cause you—and others—considerable inconvenience. At this point you do not have much choice if you are to impress on her the importance of completing homework. Perhaps you have a family event coming up, or she is eagerly anticipating a social event with her friends. Let her know that the upcoming event, whatever it is, will be postponed until she can show responsibility for her homework. Clarify what responsibility in this case means. It could be something like completing five consecutive days of homework. If this inconveniences family or friends, remember it will only be a short-term inconvenience for a long-term gain.

Mealtime Routine

- Select and name the routine: mealtime routine.
- Identify routine boundaries: breakfast and dinner (if you are home all day, include lunch).
- Identify the basic steps: sit down at the table when the meal is ready, finish your meal before leaving the table, help clear the dishes.

Go through the rest of the setup process and try out the first version of your mealtime routine. The most common problems during mealtime routines are picky eaters, dawdlers, and those who leave the table before finishing. Mealtimes provide a great opportunity to let natural consequences (hunger) shape your child's behavior. All you have to do is get prepared, set the wheels in motion, and let reality work for you. If you are like most parents, your kitchen is not open for business twenty-four hours a day, and you do not have a daily menu with multiple selections. However, if you are the parent of a picky eater, you may certainly *feel* like you are running a restaurant instead of a household. Since providing food is a parent's most fundamental job, withholding it (the cure for picky eating) can be emotionally difficult for you. So, before you make a change, resolve any qualms you have about withholding a meal or a couple of snacks. Here are three typical mealtime problems:

- **The Interrupter** has a habit of picking at her food, going to play with something, coming back for more picking, and going off again. Completing her meal takes ages, and you dislike nagging her to finish.
- **The Grazer** rarely finishes an entire meal or snack and seems to be constantly nibbling on something.
- **The Selector** will only eat two or three foods and will not try anything else.

Solutions for the poor eating habits described above can be found in The End of Picky Eating in Chapter 7.

Evening and Bedtime Routine

- Select and name the routine: evening and bedtime routine.
- Identify routine boundaries: between dinner and going to sleep.
- Identify the basic steps: picking up toys, quiet activity, bath, dress for bed, brush teeth, get into bed, story time.

Go through the rest of the setup process and try out the first version. The most common problems during this routine are: behaviors that are affected by tiredness; scrambling to attend to the day's unfinished business or to prepare for the next day; participating in stimulating rather than calming activities; staying up too late, and not staying in bed.

To make the evening routine run smoothly, stay calm, keep activities short and relaxing, and put your child to bed on time—earlier if necessary but not later. At the end of a long day, everyone is tired, and poor behaviors thrive under such conditions. If your child is wiped out most nights after dinner and is only half an hour away from bedtime, have her pick up her toys before dinner. When dinner is over, and she has helped clean up (if she is old enough), you may allow her to indulge in a quiet activity she enjoys. If bath time is next on the agenda, move on to that activity and remind or encourage her to join in if she is not already involved. If she misses her bath, move on to the next part of the routine: putting on pajamas, brushing teeth, getting into bed, and story time.

If she resists brushing her teeth before bed--which is a common complaint—you cannot comfortably ignore it, since teeth have to be cleaned. Include something in the bedtime routine that she likes, such as reading with you, or watching a short video or television show. When she brushes her teeth, she gets the activity she likes. If she does not brush her teeth, she goes to bed without it. Tell her she can have that activity again the next night if she has her teeth brushed in time.

As additional motivation—should your child need it—tell her that unbrushed teeth are unprotected teeth, and until they are protected she will not be allowed to eat or drink anything sugary.

Establishing routines for these common family activities can be enormously helpful, and worth all the time and attention you spend on their preparation. Working on them with the first child at the beginning of your parenting career will yield great benefits down the road with additional children. Start as soon as possible, and enjoy the calm.

CHAPTER 9

CONCLUSION

When I set out to write this book, my goal was to fill—in a small way—what I see as a tremendous gap in our schools and colleges: education and training on relationships, and preparation for parenting. My dream is to one day see (and in the meantime influence to the best of my ability) legislation that encourages and supports comprehensive relationship and parenting education at all levels of schooling. I am not alone in thinking many of our social ills are caused by a lack of knowledge on how to parent well, but thus far our collective angst has not had enough impact to change those societal ills through improved preparedness and skill development. Perhaps I will not see a huge change in my lifetime, but I can make a difference in a few parents' lives. I hope I have done that for you with this book and that now you are a different, more confident and effective, parent than you were when you opened it.

The author with her granddaughter Lily Rose
who inspired this book and to whom it is dedicated.